Warrior
A Man's Guide to Spiritual Power and Purpose

Warrior
A Man's Guide to Spiritual Power and Purpose

By Caleb Elias Hart

© 2025 Caleb Elias Hart
All rights reserved.

No part of this publication may be reproduced, stored in a retrieval system, or transmitted in any form or by any means - electronic, mechanical, photocopying, recording, or otherwise - without the prior written permission of the author, except for brief quotations used in reviews or scholarly works. Copies are allowed for pages where permission is explicitly given in the book.

Unless otherwise noted, all Scripture quotations are taken from the **New International Version® (NIV®)** of the Holy Bible, © 1973, 1978, 1984, 2011 by Biblica, Inc.™ Used by permission. All rights reserved worldwide.

Some Scripture quotations may also be taken from the **New Living Translation (NLT)** of the Holy Bible, © 1996, 2004, 2015 by Tyndale House Foundation. Used by permission of Tyndale House Publishers, Inc., Carol Stream, Illinois 60188. All rights reserved.

ISBN: 978-1-968110-06-2

First Edition

Printed in the United States of America

For more information, contact: calebeliashart@gmail.com

Warrior: A Man's Guide to Spiritual Power and Purpose

Table of Contents

Preface 1
Why Men Matter in God's Kingdom 3
How to Use This Book 9
Part I Foundation of Spiritual Growth 13
    Chapter 1 The Identity of a Godly Man 15
    Chapter 2 The Authority of God's Word 24
    Chapter 3 The Power of the Cross 29
Part II Building Strong Spiritual Disciplines 37
    Chapter 4 Prayer That Moves Mountains 40
    Chapter 5 Fasting and Spiritual Focus 53
    Chapter 6 The Power of Worship and Praise 59
    Chapter 7 Walking in Obedience 65
Part III Battling for Holiness and Victory 71
    Chapter 8 Spiritual Warfare 101 73
    Chapter 9 Overcoming Temptation 81
    Chapter 10 Freedom from Strongholds 91
Part IV Leading and Impacting with Power 101
    Chapter 11 The Role of a Spiritual Leader 103
    Chapter 12 Discipleship and Brotherhood 115
    Chapter 13 Living a Missional Life 126
Part V Perseverance and Legacy 136
    Chapter 14 Standing Firm in Trials 138
    Chapter 15 Finishing the Race Well 149
Conclusion Empowered for a Life that Honors God 155
A Final Charge to Men of Faith 157
Afterword 159

Appendices 160
   APPENDIX: 90-Day Bible Reading Plan 160
   APPENDIX: Accepting Christ 166
   APPENDIX: Prayers 173

Preface

There has never been a more urgent time for men to rise up in strength, truth, and spiritual power.

We live in a world that's confused about manhood, dismissive of truth, and increasingly hostile to faith. Too many men are stuck, spiritually passive, isolated, discouraged, or defeated. I believe, with everything in me, that God is calling men back, not to religion and not to performance, but to a deep, authentic, Spirit-empowered relationship with Jesus Christ.

That's why this book matters. It speaks directly to the deep need in men today and calls them into the kind of faith that's not empty, passive, or performance-based, but bold, disciplined, and fully alive.

Warrior: A Man's Guide to Spiritual Power and Purpose isn't another self-help manual or a list of religious checkboxes. It's a call to arms and a challenge to men to step into their God-given identity, to cultivate strength through discipline, to walk in purity, lead with humility, and finish life with faithfulness and fire.

The message here is grounded in Scripture, forged through real life, and delivered with clarity and conviction. Every chapter points men back to the source of their strength. That source is Jesus. Each chapter is also to call men higher and to equip them.

I've had the honor of walking with many men over the years, including leaders, fathers, sons, brothers, mentors, and warriors. The ones who make it, the ones who grow, overcome, and lead well, are not always the most gifted, but they are humble, teachable, committed, and surrendered. If that's your heart, this book is for you.

Read it slowly, reflect honestly, take action deliberately, and don't go alone. This book is best walked out with brothers in Christ, that is, with men who will sharpen you, challenge you, and grow with you.

I believe the truths in this book can change your life. You will be able to benefit yourself and the generations that come after you.

Let's not settle for being men of convenience, opinion, and comfort.

Let's become men of character, conviction, and courage.

Let's grow, lead, fight, and let's finish well, for the glory of God.

Why Men Matter in God's Kingdom

God created men with purpose and on purpose. From the very beginning, He placed Adam in the garden to enjoy it, but also to lead, protect, and cultivate it. Since God does not make accidents, that was intentional then, and it still is.

Men today are facing a quiet crisis. Many feel spiritually passive, unsure of their role, or disconnected from God's calling on their lives. Culture sends mixed signals about masculinity, but God's Word is clear: men are called to be strong in spirit, humble in heart, courageous in action, and grounded in truth. There is no intention or need to be perfect, but only to be present, obedient, and faithful.

God is still looking for men who will stand up and take their place in His Kingdom. Men who aren't afraid to follow Jesus boldly, lead their families with love and integrity, and live lives shaped by Scripture, not the culture around them. Ezekiel 22:30 (NIV) says, *"I looked for someone among them who would build up the wall and stand before me in the gap on behalf of the land... but I found no one."* That verse is a challenge, but also a call: Will we be the men who stand in the gap?

God's Design for Men is Good

You matter to God, of course, because you exist, and also because He designed you for impact. You were created with spiritual authority and responsibility.

In Genesis 2:15, Adam is given work, purpose, and a command. That pattern continues throughout Scripture: Noah built, Abraham obeyed, Moses led, Joshua fought, David worshipped, and Paul preached. Each of these men had flaws, but they also had faith. God used them because they were willing to respond.

I heard one minister in the faith often say, "God is not interested in your ability, but in your availability!". There's no shortage of brokenness in the world. Families are fractured. Communities are struggling. Churches are weakening. When men pursue spiritual growth and walk in God's power, things change.

The enemy works hard to keep men distracted, discouraged, and spiritually disengaged because he knows what's at stake. Spiritually equipped men are a threat to darkness.

You Are Called to More

This book is about growth and power, specifically, spiritual power that comes from a relationship with Jesus, shaped by Scripture, and strengthened by the Holy Spirit. We will investigate becoming the kind of man who hears God's voice and obeys it. The kind of man who knows how to pray, how to lead, how to fight spiritual battles, and how to leave a legacy of faith.

If you've ever felt like your spiritual life is stuck or like you're meant for more, then this is a good sign. That's the Holy Spirit nudging you forward. This journey is for men who are tired of standing on the sidelines and are ready to step into the life God created them to live.

Your presence matters. Your prayers matter. Your leadership matters, and your growth matters. You matter to your family, your church, your community, and the Kingdom of God.

The Call to Spiritual Growth and Power

God is not calling you to a life of passive faith. He's calling you to grow strong, stand firm, and live with power. Spiritual growth isn't just for pastors, missionaries, or men who seem to "have it all together." It's for every man who calls Jesus Lord.

If you belong to Christ, then you've been enlisted in a spiritual battle (Ephesians 6:10-13). Whether you feel ready or not, the fight is already happening. The fight is not a fight against people, but a fight for your heart, your mind, your family, your integrity, your legacy, and your faith. Growth and strength in this fight don't come from trying harder. These come from walking daily with God and letting His Spirit shape you.

Growing in Christ Is Necessary

You were saved to grow strong and not to sit still. Growth is necessary for all life. You are either growing or dying.

2 Peter 3:18 (NIV) commands us: *"But grow in the grace and knowledge of our Lord and Savior Jesus Christ. To him be glory both now and forever! Amen."*

That's not a casual suggestion but a direct call to action. For the man who claims to follow Christ, growth is evidence of life, health, and surrender.

Too many men settle for belief without transformation. This looks like attending church, nodding at sermons, and then drifting through life unchanged. Surface-level faith won't hold up when temptation hits, when the family needs a leader, or when life drops you to your knees. Weak faith folds under pressure. Real growth is what makes you resilient, rooted, and ready.

Growth won't happen by accident. It takes humility to admit you need it. It takes discipline to pursue it. It takes brotherhood to sustain it. The result is worth it: clarity in confusion, courage in trials, power in prayer, and conviction in how you lead, love, and live.

God is not calling you to be religious. He's calling you to be dangerous to the darkness, and that starts with real, consistent, spiritual growth.

Real Power Comes from God

Power in God's Kingdom isn't about domination; it's about submission. It's not about being the loudest in the room or the strongest in the gym. It's about being surrendered to the Holy Spirit and walking in the authority Christ gives you.

Acts 1:8 (NLT) says, *"But you will receive power when the Holy Spirit comes upon you. And you will be my witnesses…"* That word *power* is **dynamis** in Greek, and it's where we get the word *dynamite*.

This isn't personality power or willpower. It's spiritual power. And it's available to every believer who seeks God, obeys His Word, and yields to His Spirit.

The world needs men who are spiritually awake. Men who are wise and grounded. Men who aren't swayed by trends, politics, or pressure. Men who stand tall because they kneel often. That kind of strength comes only from God, and it's cultivated through growth.

This Is Your Invitation

You have probably seen Christian rules and ToDos, but in this book, you are invited to grow strong by being equipped to pursue Christ with purpose and by building a relationship. Each chapter will give you clear truth from God's Word, practical steps you can take, and challenges to push you forward.

You don't have to figure it all out before you start. Just start. You've already opened this book. Now, open your

Bible, open your heart, and show up to the process. Trust that God will meet you there.

The Kingdom of God doesn't need more passive or distracted men. It needs men who are equipped for the fight;

Men who know their identity in Christ and are trained to walk in spiritual authority.

Men who are grounded in Scripture, led by the Holy Spirit, and mature in character.

Men who are equipped with discernment to spot deception, wisdom to make sound decisions, courage to stand for truth, humility to serve, and faith to obey when it's hard.

Men who know how to pray with power, lead their families, fight against temptation, and build up others.

Men who carry the presence of God into their homes, their workplaces, their churches, and wherever God assigns them.

This kind of man is built through surrender, discipline, and a deep connection with Jesus Christ. Your next step is growth. Your source is Jesus and God's Word. Your time is now.

How to Use This Book

This book isn't something you simply read and set aside. It's meant to be processed, prayed through, and put into action. *Warrior: A Man's Guide to Spiritual Power and Purpose* was written to help you become the man God designed you to be, growing one step at a time through truth, reflection, and obedience.

Whether you're reading this alone or with other men, here's how to get the most from it:

1. Go Thru One Chapter at a Time

Don't rush. Each chapter is designed to challenge, stretch, and strengthen you. Take time to reflect on the biblical truths, personal applications, and questions that come up. Growth happens in the process, not in the speed.

2. Bring Your Sword (the Bible)

This book is grounded in Scripture. Keep your Bible nearby and look up the verses referenced throughout each chapter. Let God's Word speak directly to your heart, more than anything written here ever could.

3. Journal What God Shows You

Growth sticks when it's processed. Use a notebook or journal to write down:

- What stood out to you
- What God is showing you
- What do you feel challenged to change or obey
- Prayers, breakthroughs, or moments of conviction

---

4. Engage the Study Guide

Each chapter has a companion study guide section with:

- A key verse to memorize or meditate on
- A brief summary of the main theme
- Discussion/reflection questions
- A practical weekly challenge to apply what you've learned

Use it on your own, with a brother, or in a men's group. This is where truth moves from theory to transformation.

---

5. Commit to Growth, Not Perfection

Take perfection off the table. You don't need to have it all together to start. This book isn't about performing for God. It's about walking with Him. Be honest. Be humble. Stay hungry. Let grace carry you forward as you become stronger in spirit and more confident in your calling.

6. Share the Journey

If this book speaks to you, don't keep it to yourself. Invite other men into the process. Use it to discuss, disciple, encourage, and equip someone else. We grow stronger together.

You were never meant to live a passive, distracted, or defeated life.

This book is here to help you break free from what's been holding you back and step into the spiritual strength, clarity, and purpose God designed for you.

Let's get to work.

Part I
Foundation of Spiritual Growth

Becoming the Man God Has Already Declared You to Be

Before you can build anything strong, a solid foundation is needed. That's true in construction, and it's just as true in your spiritual life. If you want to be a man of strength, integrity, purity, and purpose, you need to build on something that's stable, unchanging, and true.

That foundation is found in your identity in Christ, the authority of God's Word, and the finished work of the cross.

Too many men try to grow spiritually without first settling who they are, what they stand for, and what's already been done for them. They chase spiritual activity while ignoring spiritual reality. Strength doesn't come from striving; it comes from standing on the truth.

In Part 1, you'll lay that foundation. These first three chapters are not lightweight. They are core. If you miss this part, everything else will eventually crack under pressure, including prayer, leadership, discipline, and purity.

Here's what this section will help you do:

- **Chapter 1: The Identity of a Godly Man** will help you stop living under false labels and start living from your true identity in Christ. You'll learn what God says about you and how to walk in that truth every day.

- **Chapter 2: The Authority of God's Word** will remind you that Scripture is your ultimate source of truth, direction, and spiritual power. You'll learn how to read it for knowledge and for transformation.

- **Chapter 3: The Power of the Cross** will shift your mindset from striving to trusting. You'll discover that indeed the cross is where your sins were forgiven, and it's also where your strength begins and shame ends.

These truths are more than theological concepts, so consider them as your spiritual weapons. When you understand who you are, where you stand, and what's already been won for you, you stop living like a servant and start living like a son.

Don't rush this part. Don't skip the foundation. Let these chapters reset your mindset, rebuild your confidence, and ignite your pursuit of spiritual growth with clarity and conviction. You can't build a strong life on a weak foundation. When your foundation is built on truth, you can grow into the man God has called you to be. You become steady, resilient, and able to build a life that lasts.

Chapter 1
The Identity of a Godly Man

Understanding Your Identity in Christ

Before we talk about spiritual disciplines or leadership or overcoming sin, we have to start with identity. Why? Because what you believe about yourself shapes how you live.

If you don't know who you are in Christ, you'll spend your life trying to earn approval, prove your worth, or hide your failures, but when you know who you are, and I mean really know it, then everything changes.

Every man wrestles with the question, *"Do I have what it takes?"* It manifests in how we conduct our day-to-day activities, such as how we lead, work, and interact with others, as well as how we approach God.

The world throws its own answers at us: You're only as good as your bank account. You're only valuable if you perform. You're only a real man if you never show weakness.

These lies run deep and can be highly destructive. Over time, they can distort our perception of ourselves and our understanding of God's view of us.

God is not interested in shallow religion or a faith based on performance. He is interested in who you are becoming and building a relationship with Him. He wants to transform you from the inside out.

transformation starts when you understand your identity in Christ. This means, not in the world's eyes, not in your own strength, but in Christ.

The Bible doesn't just tell us what to do; it tells us who we are. In fact, God often reminds people of their identity *before* He gives them a task:

- To Gideon, who was hiding in fear, God said, *"The Lord is with you, mighty warrior"* (Judges 6:12 NIV).

- To Peter, the impulsive fisherman, Jesus said, *"You are Peter, and on this rock I will build my church"* (Matthew 16:18 NIV).

- To Jesus at His baptism before any miracles or ministry, God said, *"This is my Son, whom I love; with him I am well pleased"* (Matthew 3:17 NIV).

God defines identity before He calls you into mission, and the same is true for you.

If you skip this chapter or rush through it, the rest of the book will feel like pressure instead of power. You'll try to grow spiritually without understanding the grace and identity that make that growth possible. That's like trying to build a house without a foundation. It is sure to fall.

So, be sure to slow down here. Let truth settle in your spirit. In this chapter, you will get more than head knowledge. You will understand heart alignment and embrace the reality that you are no longer the person you used to be. You are not your failures. You are not what others have spoken over you. You are a new creation, defined by the One who made you, redeemed you, and calls you His own.

You Are a Son, Not Just a Servant

One of the most important truths you can settle in your heart is this: you are not just a servant of God, you are His son. Yes, we serve Him and we honor Him, but our relationship with Him is not built on performance or duty. It's built on love, adoption, and a sense of belonging.

Galatians 4:6-7 (NIV) says,

"Because you are his sons, God sent the Spirit of his Son into our hearts, the Spirit who calls out, 'Abba, Father.' So you are no longer a slave, but God's child; and since you are his child, God has made you also an heir."

This changes everything.

A servant works for acceptance. A son lives from it.
A servant fears being dismissed. A son knows he belongs.
A servant obeys out of obligation. A son obeys out of love.

You don't approach God as a distant ruler, hoping you've done enough to be heard. You come to Him as your Father. You are welcomed and wanted. You are fully known and fully loved.

This identity as a son shapes how you pray, how you lead, how you repent, and how you grow. It gives you stability when life is uncertain. It gives you boldness when you're tempted to hide. It reminds you that your place in God's family is not based on your performance but on His grace.

Some think of God as the grey-haired papa who looks for and waits for you to mess up, but that is not the case. A papa, yes, waiting for you to mess up, not at all. It is like a father loving his son. You do not have to perform or achieve for Him to love you.

When you forget you're a son, you start living like a spiritual orphan driven by pressure, performing for approval, or withdrawing in shame. When you remember who you are, you live differently. You walk with confidence, you draw near to God, and you rise when you fall.

You are a son of God. That's a position you've been given through Jesus Christ, and when you truly believe that, you begin to live like it.

This is your identity.
This is your foundation.
This is where godly strength begins.

Once you know who you are, you can begin to live like the godly man you were created to be.

Let's examine some scripture verses and gain a deeper understanding of them.

Scripture References

(2 Corinthians 5:17, Galatians 2:20)

Knowing who you are in Christ changes everything. It shapes how you think, how you live, how you lead, and how you fight. Without a clear sense of identity, a man can go through life unsure, insecure, or constantly striving for validation. But when your identity is rooted in Christ, you walk in confidence, not arrogance. You walk with the assurance that comes from being grounded in truth.

2 Corinthians 5:17 (NIV) says, *"Therefore, if anyone is in Christ, the new creation has come: The old has gone, the new is here!"*

That's not a metaphor. That's a spiritual reality. When you put your faith in Jesus, you're not just a slightly better version of your old self—you're new. Fully accepted, fully forgiven, fully empowered. You are not defined by your past, your mistakes, your job, or your background. You are defined by Christ.

Galatians 2:20 (NIV) reinforces this truth: *"I have been crucified with Christ and I no longer live, but Christ lives in me. The life I now live in the body, I live by faith in the Son of God, who loved me and gave himself for me."*

That verse, though more than good theology, is a blueprint for how a godly man lives: surrendered, Spirit-filled, and fully committed to Jesus.

A godly man doesn't earn his identity; he receives it. Your worth comes from the finished work of Christ and your position in Him.

Breaking Free from the World's Labels

The world is quick to label men. You're only successful if you make enough money. You're only valuable if you're physically strong, in control, or admired. Failures become identities. Wounds become narratives. The enemy uses those labels to keep men stuck, ashamed, or constantly trying to prove something, but God speaks a better word over you.

You are:

- **Chosen** - (1 Peter 2:9)
  "But you are a chosen people, a royal priesthood, a holy nation, God's special possession..."
- **Adopted** - (Ephesians 1:5)
  "He predestined us for adoption to sonship through Jesus Christ, in accordance with His pleasure and will..."
- **Redeemed** - (Colossians 1:13-14)
  "For He has rescued us from the dominion of darkness and brought us into the kingdom of the Son He loves, in whom we have redemption, the forgiveness of sins."
- **Forgiven** - (1 John 1:9)
  "If we confess our sins, He is faithful and just and will forgive us our sins and purify us from all unrighteousness."
- **More Than a Conqueror** - (Romans 8:37)
  "In all these things we are more than conquerors through Him who loved us."
- **God's Workmanship** - (Ephesians 2:10)
  "For we are God's workmanship, created in Christ Jesus to do good works, which God prepared in advance for us to do."

- **A New Creation** - (2 Corinthians 5:17)
  "Therefore, if anyone is in Christ, the new creation has come: The old has gone, the new is here!"
- **A Temple of the Holy Spirit** - (1 Corinthians 6:19-20)
  "Do you not know that your bodies are temples of the Holy Spirit... You are not your own; you were bought at a price."
- **An Heir of God** - (Romans 8:17)
  "Now if we are children, then we are heirs—heirs of God and co-heirs with Christ..."
- **Free Indeed** - (John 8:36)
  "So if the Son sets you free, you will be free indeed."

When God looks at you, He doesn't see a failure or a fraud. He sees a son and not just any son, but one who is redeemed, chosen, deeply loved, and righteous through Christ. You are called with purpose, equipped with power, and positioned for the good works God prepared specifically for you (Ephesians 2:10) *"For we are God's handiwork, created in Christ Jesus to do good works, which God prepared in advance for us to do."*

That's not hype. That's truth.

The real questions are these:

Will you believe it?

Will you stop living under the weight of old labels, past wounds, and silent shame?

Will you start agreeing with what God says about you, even when your feelings or your history say something else?

Breaking free from false identity is not a one-time decision. It's a daily mindset shift. It's waking up each day and choosing truth over lies, sonship over striving, and confidence over condemnation. As Romans 12:2 commands, let your mind be transformed, not conformed to the patterns of this world, but renewed through God's Word.

You will still hear the voices. The world will try to define you by your success, your failure, your past, or your performance. The enemy will whisper that you're not enough, not worthy, or not capable, but you have a choice. You can agree with the noise, or you can anchor yourself in what God has already declared.

You are not what you've done. You are not what others have said. You are not the mistakes you regret or the insecurities you carry.

You are who God says you are.

When you believe that, everything begins to change.

This chapter was never intended to boost your self-esteem but to awaken you to your true identity in Christ. When you know who you are, you stop living like a slave and start walking like a son. You stop striving for approval and start living from the approval already given to you in Jesus.

This is your foundation.

Before we talk about discipline, leadership, or spiritual power, you must be rooted in this truth: You belong to God. Your identity is settled. Your future is secure. Your strength begins here. Now speak it, own it, and live like it. Let's declare the truth together.

Here's a simple practice:

Every morning, declare who you are in Christ out loud. Even if you don't feel it, speak it. Over time, truth sinks in and reshapes how you think and live.

If you do not have a declaration of your own, you can start with the one given below. Feel free to modify and expand it over time as you gain more knowledge.

Daily Identity Declaration

Today, I stand in the truth of who I am in Christ.

I am **chosen** by God.
I am **adopted** as His son.
I am **redeemed** and **forgiven**, not defined by my past.
I am **a new creation**; the old me is gone.
I am **more than a conqueror** through Christ who loves me.
I am **God's workmanship**, created for a purpose.
I am **a temple of the Holy Spirit** because God lives in me.
I am **an heir of God** with a secure future.
I am **the light of the world**, called to make an impact.
I am **free indeed** because Jesus has set me free.

I don't live by the world's labels.
I don't answer to shame, fear, or failure.
I live by the truth of God's Word.
I walk in grace, strength, and purpose.

Today, I choose to believe what God says about me and I will live like it. In Jesus' name, Amen.

A Godly Man is a New Man

A godly man isn't perfect. He doesn't have it all figured out. He is not expected to have it all together. He is the kind of man who knows where his strength comes from. When he falls, he does not stay down. He gets back up because God's grace holds him, and Jesus continues to lead him.

He does not rely on the approval of others. He does not live in pride, and he refuses to carry shame. His identity is secure, not because of anything he has earned, but because of what Christ has already done. That is the power of grace, and it gives you a new name, a new standing, and a new way to live.

This is where spiritual growth truly begins. Focus on the right identity. When you know who you are in Christ, everything else begins to fall into place. Your decisions, your habits, your relationships, and your leadership will all flow from that core truth.

You are not your past. You are not your failures. You are a new creation. If you forget who you are, everything else begins to drift.

When you stay rooted in your identity as a son of God, you become strong, steady, and ready for the life God is calling you to live.

You are a new creation in Christ. The old is gone, and the new is here. Now it's time to build your life on that truth.

The place to start building? The Word of God.

Chapter 2
The Authority of God's Word

Every man is being shaped by something. You are being formed, right now, by the voices you listen to, the habits you keep, and the truths you believe. The question is: What's your source?

There's no shortage of input. Podcasts, articles, news, influencers, opinions, social media, and trends. We're surrounded by noise, but spiritual strength doesn't come from noise. It comes from anchoring your life to truth that doesn't waver.

If you want to grow strong spiritually, you need a foundation that's stronger than your circumstances and deeper than your emotions. You need the Word of God.

Most men know they should read the Bible, but for many, it becomes a box to check, something they feel guilty for not doing, or something they only reach for when life falls apart. For others, it takes a back seat to all the day-to-day activities. We don't want to take you on a guilt trip. We want you to understand the profound importance of the Word of God, which serves as your source of strength, clarity, and direction in a world full of confusion and compromise.

Here's the truth: You cannot become spiritually strong apart from Scripture. It's not possible. God didn't design your life to run on momentum, emotion, or motivational quotes. He designed it to run on His Word. The Bible isn't just helpful, it's holy and powerful. It was breathed out by God Himself.

In 2 Timothy 3:16, God reveals the explanation of the Word as His character, His promises, His will, and His commands.

"All Scripture is God-breathed and is useful for teaching, rebuking, correcting and training in righteousness, "

It equips you for every challenge, trains you for every good work, and grounds you when everything else is shifting.

Jesus modeled this perfectly. When Satan tempted Him in the wilderness, Jesus didn't argue or rationalize.

He quoted Scripture (Matthew 4). Here's something we often overlook: Satan also quoted Scripture and twisted it for his own purposes.

---

*This is a critical warning:
Knowing the Bible isn't enough.
Satan knows it, too.*

If you don't align with Christ and obey what the Word says, you're still vulnerable. The authority of Scripture doesn't come from merely knowing it–it comes from living under it.

It is essential for you to transition from occasional Bible reading (or no Bible reading) to a life anchored in biblical living.

We'll explore how the Word forms your worldview, trains your conscience, and equips you to lead with wisdom. We'll get practical about how to make time in the Word, a non-negotiable, consistent, life-giving daily life rhythm, even with a busy schedule.

The goal isn't to become a Bible expert.

The goal is to become a man who **knows the Word, lives the Word, and is led by the Word.**

When you build your life on Scripture, you don't just grow, you grow strong.

Why Scripture is the Bedrock

Every man builds his life on something. Some on their past, some on pain, preferences, or pride. Some lean on emotions, others on intellect or culture. Only one foundation is strong enough to carry the weight of your life, your leadership, and your legacy: the Word of God.

"All Scripture is God-breathed and is useful for teaching, rebuking, correcting and training in righteousness, so that the servant of God may be thoroughly equipped for every good work." –2 Timothy 3:16-17 (NIV)

If you want to be equipped to lead, to fight, to endure, and to walk with God, you need Scripture regularly. You may be tempted when life gets tough. You also need it daily, because it's essential.

Think of it as a savings account. When you put money in, it is there for when it is needed. Similarly, when you put the Word into you, it's there when times are tough, when answers are not clear, and when inspiration and encouragement are needed.

It's not optional reading, reserved for pastors or spiritual elites. It's the lifeline of every man who wants to live in truth and walk in power. It's how we know right from wrong, truth from deception, and wisdom from noise. In our world filled with opinions, trends, and constantly shifting values, we need a foundation that remains unchanged. We need TRUTH, and that's the Bible.

God's Word reveals His heart, His ways, His promises, and His truth (which is the unadulterated Truth). It reveals who God is, who you are, and how to navigate a world that constantly seeks to distort all three.

When you fill your mind with truth and keep God's Word on your lips, just as Joshua was commanded, you will find strength and direction for every season.

"Keep this Book of the Law always on your lips; meditate on it day and night... Then you will be prosperous and successful." –Joshua 1:8 (NIV)

This isn't about legalism. It's about training for war and anchoring your thoughts, words, and decisions in truth that doesn't shift.

When Scripture becomes your bedrock, you become stable, strong, and ready for whatever God calls you to do. You become more than a survivor, and never a victim. You become an overcomer and a victor.

How to Read and Apply the Bible Daily

Reading the Bible strengthens your faith and equips you to face each day with clarity and courage. God's Word is your sword (Ephesians 6:17), and spending time in it prepares you to stand strong and live with purpose.

You can read multiple chapters at one time to grow, but even 10 to 15 minutes a day, with a teachable heart and an open Bible, can bring lasting change. Start small, stay consistent, and trust that God will meet you there.

Here's a simple framework for daily Scripture time:

1. Read with a purpose.
Pick a book of the Bible and read it slowly and carefully, chapter by chapter. Start with the Gospels (Matthew, Mark, Luke, or John), Proverbs, or one of Paul's letters like Ephesians or Philippians.

2. Ask three questions:

- *What does this teach me about God?*
- *What does this reveal about myself?*
- *How should I respond today?*

3. Pray what you read.
Turn Scripture into prayer. If you read about God's faithfulness, thank Him for it. If the Word challenges your sin, confess and ask for strength. You want to build your relationship while you're gaining information.

4. Obey what you learn.
James 1:22 says, *"Do not merely listen to the word, and so deceive yourselves. Do what it says."*

Treat the bible like a guide for your life. Apply one truth at a time.

Make God's Word Your Standard

The man who lives by Scripture doesn't get tossed around by emotions, culture, or compromise. He's steady. He knows how to respond in chaos. He knows how to lead when things get tough. He knows how to discern what's real from what just sounds spiritual.

This chapter provides a path for you. When the Bible becomes your foundation, you become grounded, wise, and equipped for every good work.

God wants to speak to you every day. The question is, will you meet Him in His Word?

Chapter 3
The Power of the Cross

Building spiritual strength requires understanding where that strength comes from. It doesn't come from trying harder, being more disciplined, or stacking up good behavior. It comes from the cross.

The cross is the starting point of your salvation and the foundation of your entire spiritual life. It's where your old life ends and your new life begins. It's where sin was crushed, shame was removed, and access to God was fully opened by the tearing of the veil to the Holy of Holies, which is where God's presence was. Because of this, we now have access to the Father through the Son, since He was raised from the dead.

Luke 23:44-47 New King James Version (NKJV)Now it was about the sixth hour, and there was darkness over all the earth until the ninth hour. Then the sun was darkened, and the veil of the temple was torn in two. And when Jesus had cried out with a loud voice, He said, "Father, into Your hands I commit My spirit.

Learn more about the veil being torn here:
https://www.gotquestions.org/temple-veil-torn.html

Every godly man must return to the cross again and again. Why? Because slipping back into legalism, performance, pressure, and self-reliance is easy, even as believers.

We believe spiritual growth means working our way into God's favor, but it's not possible, and that's not the gospel. The gospel is this: Jesus already did the work. He lived the sinless life you couldn't live, died the death you deserved, and rose from the grave to offer you forgiveness, freedom, and new life.

Your job is to trust what He has done, walk in that truth daily, and live from the grace He freely gives.

"But God demonstrates his own love for us in this: While we were still sinners, Christ died for us." –Romans 5:8 (NIV)

Since you cannot earn your way to God, focus on receiving what He has already done for you through Jesus. That is the power of the cross.

Paul understood this well. In 1 Corinthians 2:2 (NIV), he said, *"For I resolved to know nothing while I was with you except Jesus Christ and him crucified."* That was his deliberate choice to keep the cross at the center of everything because once you move away from the cross, you start operating in your own strength, and eventually, you burn out.

In this chapter, we're going to slow down and look at what actually happened at the cross, not just physically, but spiritually. We'll unpack the finished work of Christ and what it means for you today, in your mind, in your struggles, in your freedom, and in how you view yourself before God.

We'll also talk about real grace. Not the kind of grace that gets misused as an excuse for sin, but the kind that leads to real change, because when you know you're forgiven, things change. They change because you know you're accepted, you stop hiding, and you stop striving. When you live from grace instead of guilt, you actually start growing. Spiritual growth is the key!

This is fuel for your everyday life. Your past doesn't have the final word, your shame doesn't have to define you, and your struggles don't have to own you. Why? Because the cross has already spoken: You are free. You are forgiven. You are His.

If you can get this deep down inside, you'll stop chasing identity, stop fearing failure, and start walking in the power that comes from what Jesus already accomplished.

It all starts at the cross. And it's where we return every day to be reminded: It is finished.

In case you are not already a Christ follower, at the end of this book, we explain what it means to be a Christ follower and how to give your life to the Lord.

Christ's Finished Work

At the center of the Christian life is the cross, which is the place where everything changed, when sin was defeated, shame was broken, and new life was made possible.

Colossians 2:13-15 (NIV) says, *"When you were dead in your sins and in the uncircumcision of your flesh, God made you alive with Christ. He forgave us all our sins, having canceled the charge of our legal indebtedness... He has taken it away, nailing it to the cross. And having disarmed the powers and authorities, He made a public spectacle of them, triumphing over them by the cross."*

Jesus didn't die to make you slightly better. He died to make you fully alive. The cross is where your old self died and where your freedom began. When Jesus said, *"It is finished,"* in John 19:30, He meant that the debt was paid, the guilt was lifted, and the enemy was disarmed.

You don't have to carry shame anymore, you don't have to earn forgiveness, and you don't have to wonder if God's love for you is secure because the cross proved it.

This truth is the foundation of spiritual growth. If you skip over the cross, you'll spend your life trying to fix what Jesus already finished, but if you stay rooted in the power of the cross, you'll grow in grace, rather than in guilt.

Living in Grace, Not Guilt or Shame

Every man carries something. For some, it's guilt or regret over things you've done, people you've hurt, or sin you still hide. For others, it's shame, not just over your actions, but over who you believe you've become. When we're honest, most of us carry both. Guilt says, "You messed up." Shame whispers, "You are a mess." These voices can be loud, and the enemy uses them to keep men spiritually stuck, emotionally guarded, and distant from God, but the cross changes everything.

Romans 8:1 (NIV) says, *"Therefore, there is now no condemnation for those who are in Christ Jesus."*

This is a legal and spiritual declaration. When you belong to Jesus, your guilt has been removed, and your shame has been silenced. You are not condemned. You are forgiven, accepted, and deeply loved by your Father.

This truth is an invitation to live free. Paul makes it clear several times in Romans that God's grace is not permission to sin. It is the power to change.

As Titus 2:11-12 says, *"For the grace of God has appeared that offers salvation to all people. It teaches us to say 'No' to ungodliness and worldly passions, and to live self-controlled, upright and godly lives..."*

Grace trains you. It helps you grow strong and steady as you follow Christ.

When you are a believer:

You don't obey to earn God's love because you already have it.

You don't change to get close to God because you already are.

Stop letting guilt define your spiritual life and who you are in Christ. Stop carrying shame like it's part of your identity. The cross, in addition to your behavior, dealt with your burden, too.

Guilt paralyzes, shame isolates, but grace restores. You grow when you stand in grace. You grow, not by trying harder, but by trusting deeper.

Your Strength Starts at the Cross

Everything you need for spiritual growth, including freedom, peace, strength, and purpose, flows from the cross. That's where your new identity began, that's where your past lost its power, and that's where your spiritual authority was restored.

When you feel stuck or weighed down, come back to the cross. When you mess up, come back to the cross. When you forget who you are, come back to the cross, because the cross is the source of your strength every day.

How to Become a Follower of Christ

The power of the cross is more than just a concept to understand; it's an invitation to respond. If you've been reading this book and wondering where you really stand with God, don't skip this moment. Everything begins at the cross.

To become a follower of Jesus means you stop trusting in yourself and start trusting fully in Him. It means you recognize that your sin separates you from God, and there's nothing you can do to earn your way back. The good news is this: Jesus already did what you couldn't.

He lived the sinless life you couldn't live, died the death your sin deserved, and He rose from the grave so you could be forgiven, free, and alive.

"But God demonstrates His own love for us in this: While we were still sinners, Christ died for us." –Romans 5:8 (NIV)

Following Jesus means turning away from sin and turning fully to Him, asking Him to forgive you, lead you, and make you new. It's not about being perfect. It's about surrender. If that's your desire, you can respond to Him right now, right where you are.

A Simple Prayer of Surrender

"Jesus, I believe You are the Son of God.
I believe You died on the cross for my sin, and You rose again.
I confess my sin, and I ask for Your forgiveness.
I surrender my life to You — my past, my present, and my future.
Come into my life. Make me new. Be my Savior, and be my Lord.

*I choose to follow You from this day forward.
In Your name, Amen."*

Standing in the Power of the Cross

The power of the cross is that Jesus accomplished everything necessary to bring you into full relationship with God. Through His sacrifice, sin has been defeated, shame has been lifted, and you have been invited into a life of freedom and purpose. The cross is the place where your past was dealt with, and it is also the place where your new life begins.

Grace opens the door to lasting change. When you know you are forgiven, you begin to walk in confidence. When you believe you are accepted, you stop second-guessing your worth. Grace leads to growth because it frees you to pursue God with an open heart. It strengthens you to stand in truth and respond with obedience out of love.

The cross reminds you that your identity is secure. You are not defined by your failures or your struggles. You are defined by what Jesus has done. He calls you redeemed, restored, and deeply loved.

Foundation is Set, Now Build

You've gotten through the foundational pieces. Spiritual strength begins with knowing who you are in Christ. From that foundation, everything else begins to take shape. When your identity is clear, your choices become clearer. When the truth of Scripture guides your thoughts, you begin to think with wisdom and walk with clarity. When you rely on grace, you find the strength to keep moving forward even when the path is difficult.

These are the foundations of a strong life: identity in Christ, confidence in the Word of God, and a heart shaped by grace. With these in place, you are ready to grow.

What comes next is an invitation to train. You will begin building habits that strengthen your spirit and keep you connected to the God who walks with you daily.

The foundation has been set. Now it's time to build. Let's move forward with intention, with faith, and with the power that comes from walking closely with Jesus.

Part II
Building Strong Spiritual Disciplines

Training for Strength That Lasts

Building spiritual growth requires focus, intention, and the kind of consistency that builds strength over time, which is where discipline comes in.

For many men, the word discipline brings up guilt or frustration. Maybe it reminds you of what you meant to do but didn't follow through on. Maybe it feels like pressure to perform, or a checklist you've already failed at.

Consider spiritual discipline as a way to position your life to stay connected to God, grounded in truth, and strengthened to endure. Thinking about it as performance gets in the way and misleads you into darkness.

When you think of a soldier, you think about his discipline as preparation. Without training, he can't stand the pressure when it comes. The same is true for you. If you want to grow strong and stay strong, especially in a world that constantly pushes against your faith, you need consistent actions and habits in your life that keep you grounded in what is real, unchanging, and powerful.

In this section, you will be establishing habits that lead to spiritual health, clarity, and power. These disciplines won't make God love you more, but they will help you live like you're already loved, which is the truth.

Here's how we'll walk through it:

Chapter 4: Prayer That Moves Mountains

Prayer is your first move. In this chapter, you'll rediscover the power, purpose, and daily importance of prayer and its connection to God. Real men pray because real strength starts with surrender. You'll learn how to cultivate a consistent prayer life that fuels every aspect of your walk with God.

Chapter 5: Fasting and Spiritual Focus

Fasting is one of the most overlooked and misunderstood disciplines, but it is a powerful way to clear spiritual clutter and tune into God's voice. This chapter will challenge you to step away from distractions, whether food, entertainment, or noise, and pursue God with focus and hunger. Fasting's focus is not about depriving yourself. It's about training your spirit to lead over your flesh.

Chapter 6: The Power of Worship and Praise

Worship is warfare. This chapter demonstrates how praise and worship transform your perspective, uplift your spirit, and invite the presence of God into your daily life.

Worship is a spiritual weapon. It moves your heart closer to God and reminds your soul of who He is, especially when life feels heavy or uncertain.

Chapter 7: Walking in Obedience

This chapter ties it all together. The goal of spiritual discipline is obedience. Obedience is about love. Jesus said, *"If you love Me, keep My commands"* (John 14:15). A godly man hears the Word and he lives it. You'll learn how obedience builds spiritual muscle, deepens your trust in God, and shapes your character over time.

Each of these chapters builds on the other. Prayer opens your connection to God. Fasting sharpens your focus. Worship fuels your passion. Obedience strengthens your walk.

Together, they form a framework and a training ground for spiritual resilience in a culture that pulls you in every direction.

If you want a faith that endures, a life that's fruitful, and a heart that stays close to God, you'll need more than good intentions. You'll need spiritual discipline, but don't worry that you're doing it alone. The Holy Spirit is your strength, and Jesus is your example.

Let's get to work.

Chapter 4
Prayer That Moves Mountains

Rediscovering the Power of Prayer

For many men, prayer feels mysterious or even intimidating. You might wonder, *Am I doing it right? Does God really hear me? Why doesn't anything seem to happen when I pray?*

Maybe prayer has become an emergency line you only use when things go wrong, or maybe it's been reduced to a habit that feels more like routine than relationship.

Here's the truth: Prayer is not a religious exercise. Prayer is where the power is.

In Mark 11:23-24 (NIV), Jesus said, *"Truly I tell you, if anyone says to this mountain, 'Go, throw yourself into the sea,' and does not doubt in their heart but believes that what they say will happen, it will be done for them. Therefore I tell you, whatever you ask for in prayer, believe that you have received it, and it will be yours."*

Jesus was giving us a picture of what bold, faith-filled prayer can do. Mountains represent the immovable and the impossible. Jesus is saying: Nothing is too big when you bring it to God in faith.

Unfortunately, the problem is that most men don't pray like that. We pray safe prayers, small prayers or vague prayers, and when nothing happens, we stop expecting anything to happen.

Scripture calls us to something higher: persistent, confident, expectant prayer that lines up with God's will and releases His power into our lives.

Remember in the previous chapter:

This identity as a son shapes how you pray, how you lead, how you repent, and how you grow. It gives you stability when life is uncertain. It gives you boldness when you're tempted to hide. It reminds you that your place in God's family is not based on your performance but on His grace.

In this chapter, you will learn how to pray like a man who knows God and knows Him as Father, not like a man who's unsure of his standing with Him. We're going to explore what prayer really is, how to make it part of your daily life, how to pray with faith and focus, and how to stay consistent when life is busy or when God feels silent.

What Is Prayer, Really?

At its core, prayer is a relationship with God expressed in communication. It's talking to your Father and not a far-off deity, not a spiritual vending machine, not a religious formality, and he is not Santa Claus.

Jesus taught us to begin our prayers with "Our Father" (Matthew 6:9). It is with relationship that prayer begins.

You can forget about prayer being fancy words or perfect timing. Think of it as honesty, showing up, and learning to bring every part of your life, including your thoughts, struggles, hopes, fears, questions, and worship, before God with humility and trust.

Here's something that will change the way you pray: God wants to hear from you. He's not bored with your voice or your requests. He's not too busy for your you.

Proverbs 15:8 (NIV) says,

"The prayer of the upright pleases Him."

Your prayer life should become a discipline, and in all cases, it is a delight to your Father who is in Heaven.

The Priority of Prayer

Jesus prayed often, and He was the Son of God! Do you think we should do likewise?

He prayed before decisions (Luke 6:12-13).
He prayed in private (Mark 1:35).
He prayed in public (John 11:41-42).
He prayed when He was overwhelmed (Matthew 26:36-44).
He prayed on the cross (Luke 23:34, 46).

If Jesus needed prayer, we definitely do.

Prayer needs to become your first response and not your last resort. That shift happens when you make prayer a regular, daily discipline, not just an occasional reaction.

How to Build a Strong and Consistent Prayer Life

(James 5:16, Luke 18:1)

If prayer is where spiritual power begins, then it stands to reason that consistency in prayer is what keeps that power flowing consistently.

Scripture does not call us to occasional or emergency prayer. Scripture calls us to persistent, powerful, and daily connection with God.

"The prayer of a righteous man is powerful and effective."–James 5:16 (NIV)

"Then Jesus told His disciples a parable to show them that they should always pray and not give up."–Luke 18:1 (NIV)

"Pray without ceasing."–I Thessalonians 5:17 (NIV)

Some men already know the value of prayer. Others are still wondering if it really makes a difference. No matter where you are, this truth stands firm: **if you want to grow strong spiritually, prayer must become a priority.**

Prayer is where battles are fought, where your heart is aligned with God's, and where clarity, strength, and peace begin to take root. Whether you're just starting out or ready to go deeper, learning how to build a strong and consistent prayer life will shape everything about your walk with God.

So, how do you build a consistent prayer life?

1. **Set a Time and Place**
    - Just like physical training, spiritual discipline requires intentionality. If you leave prayer to whenever-you-feel-like-it, it won't happen consistently. Pick a time and place that works for your schedule–even 10-15 minutes is powerful when it's consistent.

2. **Start Simple**
    - You don't need fancy words. Just be real. Start by thanking God. Confess what's weighing you down. Ask for strength and wisdom. Lift up your family. Pray Scripture out loud. Keep it simple and honest.

3. **Use a Prayer Framework if It Helps**
    - The ACTS model is simple and effective:
        1. **A**doration - Praise God for who He is.
        2. **C**onfession - Be honest about your sin.

3. **T**hanksgiving - Thank Him for what He's done.
4. **S**upplication - Ask for what you need.

- Jesus also gave us a model in the Lord's Prayer (Matthew 6:9-13). Use it as a starting point to build your rhythm.

4. **Pray the Word**

     - Use Scripture in your prayer life. Turn verses into prayer. Example: *"Lord, You said in James 1:5 that if anyone lacks wisdom, they should ask. So I'm asking; give me wisdom in this decision today."*

5. **Write it Down**

     - Keep a prayer journal. Write your prayers, and keep track of how God answers. It builds faith and helps you stay focused.

6. **Stay Consistent, Not Perfect**

     - You won't always feel inspired. That's okay. Spiritual strength comes from consistency, not emotion. Push through dry seasons, and stay in conversation with God. Feel free to tell God of your lack of inspiration. Remember, honesty and trust are two of the keys to prayer.

A man who builds a consistent prayer life becomes a man who walks in power, clarity, and peace.

You don't have to master prayer. You just have to show up daily and trust that God is listening and responding.

Start where you are. Keep showing up.

Jesus alluded to the power of prayer, moving mountains. Prayer also strengthens your heart, aligns your perspective, and draws you closer to God.

Praying with Power and Boldness

You can pray timid prayers or you can pray prayers that shake Heaven. You want prayers that shake Heaven!

God invites you to pray with confidence:

Hebrews 4:16 (NIV) *"Let us then approach God's throne of grace with confidence, so that we may receive mercy and find grace to help us in our time of need."*

How do you pray with power?

- **Pray in faith**, trusting God's character (Hebrews 11:6).
- **Pray specifically.** Name the need. Don't be vague; be clear. (Mark 10:51)
- **Pray persistently.** Jesus told us to keep asking, seeking, and knocking (Matthew 7:7-8).
- **Pray in the Spirit.** Let the Holy Spirit guide and empower your prayers (Romans 8:26-27, Jude 1:20).
- **Pray with authority.** You are a son of God, so act like it (Luke 10:19).

When Prayer Feels Hard

There will be times when you feel dry, distracted, or disappointed. That's normal so, don't give up. Prayer is about presence and not performance. Just keep showing up. Trust God even when you can't feel Him. He's always listening.

Here's a promise you can hold onto:

"The Lord is near to all who call on Him, to all who call on Him in truth."
–Psalm 145:18 (NIV)

Become a Man of Prayer

Prayer is your lifeline. It is not just something you do, not a religious task, nor a backup plan for hard days. It is a reflection of the man you are becoming. It is your strategy in battle, your place of clarity when things are uncertain, and your source of peace when the pressure is high.

A man of prayer is a man of strength, clarity, and impact. He is not driven by fear or emotion. He is grounded in the presence of God and steady in every season because his strength comes from daily connection with his Father.

A prayerless man eventually becomes a powerless man, but a man who chooses to pray consistently, honestly, and boldly becomes strong in spirit and dangerous to the enemy.

God is not looking for performance or perfection. You just need to pray persistently. He is looking for a surrendered heart.

Start where you are. Show up daily. Talk to God about what matters most: your struggles, your responsibilities, your relationships, your decisions.

Take time to listen, and as you grow in prayer, you will learn to recognize His voice, respond to His leading, and walk more closely with Him.

Make prayer your first move, your strongest habit, and your daily breath, and not your last resort. When prayer becomes your priority, God begins to reshape your life from the inside out.

Memory Verse:

"The prayer of a righteous person is powerful and effective." –James 5:16b (NIV)

Keys to Prayer

Prayer requires intentionality. To grow strong in prayer, it is helpful to understand a few key principles that keep your heart focused, your mind engaged, and your spirit aligned with God. These are building blocks that make your time with God more meaningful and effective.

Here are five keys to strong, consistent prayer:

1. Pray with Faith

Faith is confidence in who God is and what He has promised. When you pray, trust that God hears you and responds in His wisdom and timing.

"Without faith it is impossible to please God..." (Hebrews 11:6)

2. Pray with Humility

Prayer is where you come honestly before God, acknowledging your need for Him. God resists the proud but draws near to the humble. Come as a son, not a showman.

"Humble yourselves before the Lord, and He will lift you up." (James 4:10)

3. Pray with Sincerity

God is looking for a genuine heart. Speak plainly, speak honestly, and speak often. God knows what you need before you say it, but He still wants to hear it from you.

"Pour out your hearts to Him, for God is our refuge." (Psalm 62:8)

4. Pray with Persistence

Some answers come quickly. Others take time. Don't stop praying because you don't see results right away. Keep showing up. Stay faithful. Trust that God is always working.

"Pray continually." (1 Thessalonians 5:17)

"Always pray and never give up." (Luke 18:1)

5. Pray with the Word

Praying Scripture helps align your heart with God's heart. His Word shapes your perspective, strengthens your faith, and gives language to your prayers. Let the Bible guide what you pray and how you pray.

"If you remain in me and my words remain in you, ask whatever you wish, and it will be done for you." (John 15:7)

When these keys become part of how you approach prayer, you will notice a shift. Your prayers become more focused, more honest, and more aligned with God's will. Prayer stops feeling like a task and starts becoming a place of strength, clarity, and connection with your Father, and you will enjoy being in His presence more and more.

Men grow strong in spirit by consistently and confidently showing up in prayer, trusting that God is present and working.

When Prayers Go Unanswered

Every man who takes prayer seriously will eventually face a moment of frustration, confusion, or disappointment. You pray with hope, believe God can move, and wait with expectation, but the answer doesn't come. The breakthrough doesn't happen. The silence lingers, and in that space, questions begin to rise.

You might not doubt God's power. You believe He can heal, restore, provide, or open a door. The struggle is deeper. You wonder if He will. That's where many men wrestle. We're confident in what God is able to do, but uncertain about what He is willing to do in our specific situation.

This is where faith must grow from theory to reality.

"We live by faith, not by sight." –2 Corinthians 5:7 (NIV)

Faith is more than just believing that God is capable. Faith is trusting His character when His timeline or response doesn't make sense. That doesn't mean you stop praying bold prayers. It means you hold your requests with open hands and trust God with the outcome, even if it's not what you hoped for.

There is nothing weak about asking God, "Why?", but I do not think the answer to that would be reassuring. Although Jesus did not ask, "why", even He, in the garden and on the cross, cried out in agony. He also surrendered. *"Not my will, but yours be done."* (Luke 22:42)

When your prayers go unanswered, or the answer isn't what you wanted:

- Keep praying. God sees faith in persistence, not just in passion. (Luke 18:1-8)
- Speak truth to yourself, especially when your emotions are loud.
- Lean into the Word and let it anchor your heart to what is eternal.
- Surround yourself with godly men who will stand with you and point you back to truth.
- Remember that God's silence is not His absence, and His delays are not denials.

"Though the fig tree does not bud and there are no grapes on the vines… yet I will rejoice in the Lord, I will be joyful in God my Savior."
–Habakkuk 3:17-18 (NIV)

Spiritual maturity shows up when you still pray, still believe, and still draw near to God even when you don't see what you were hoping for. That's when your faith becomes strong. That's when your relationship with God becomes deeper and more real than ever before.

God may not always answer your prayers the way you want, but He will always be faithful to walk with you, strengthen you, and shape you through the process.

So, keep trusting. Keep praying. Keep coming back to the One who knows your heart and sees the whole picture.

He is not done working.
He is not ignoring you.
And He is always good.

Declaration of Faith

I believe God is who He says He is.
I trust His power, His wisdom, and His timing.
Even when I don't see the answer, I will keep praying.
Even when I don't feel it, I know He is working.
God is faithful, and His plans for me are good.
I will walk by faith, not by sight.
My hope is in Him.

Prayer for When You're in a Season of Waiting

Father, You know the things I've been praying for.
You know the weight I carry, the questions I wrestle with, and the silence that sometimes feels heavy.
I believe You can move. I believe You are able, but in this season, I'm not sure what You're doing or when.

Still, I choose to trust You.

I surrender my timeline, my expectations, and my fears.
I lay down my need for control and open my hands again to You.
Help me to stay faithful in the waiting.
Teach me to pray with persistence and live with peace.
Remind me that Your delays are not rejections and that Your plans are still good.

Even when I don't see the outcome, help me to stay near to You.

Strengthen me today.
Guard my heart from bitterness, doubt, and discouragement.
Fill me with fresh hope, fresh faith, and the courage to keep walking.

I trust that You are with me.
I believe that You are working.
And I know You are faithful.

In Jesus' name,
Amen.

Chapter 5
Fasting and Spiritual Focus

Reclaiming the Discipline of Fasting

Fasting is one of the most neglected spiritual disciplines among Christian men, and yet one of the most powerful. For many, fasting feels extreme, uncomfortable, or confusing. Isn't that something for Old Testament prophets or super spiritual people? Why should a modern man fast?

The short answer: Jesus taught it, practiced it, and expected it.

In Matthew 6:16, Jesus said, *"When you fast…"*, not *if*. He placed fasting alongside prayer and giving as a normal part of a godly life. The early church practiced it. Jesus Himself fasted. Yet today, many believers skip this discipline entirely and miss out on the power and clarity it brings.

When you fast, you are removing distractions to increase your focus on Him. It's a deliberate choice to say, *"God, You are more important than my comfort, my habits, and even my physical needs."*

In a culture obsessed with convenience, entertainment, and constant consumption, fasting teaches self-control, sharpens your spirit, and tunes your ear to God's voice. It reminds your body that it doesn't run the show, and it reminds your spirit who truly satisfies.

In this chapter, we'll take the mystery out of fasting. You'll learn:

- What fasting is all about (and what it's not)
- Why it's important for spiritual growth
- How to fast in a healthy and biblical way
- What to expect before, during, and after a fast

- How fasting connects to breakthrough, spiritual clarity, and intimacy with God

Fasting is about alignment and giving Him your full attention, and when you do, things begin to shift.

What Is Fasting, Really?

Fasting, in this context, is voluntarily abstaining from food (or something else) for a spiritual purpose.

Biblical fasting is a spiritual discipline that helps you realign your focus on God by setting aside something physical to pursue something greater. It's not a diet or detox. It's not for the purposes of physical health, but spiritual hunger.

At its core, fasting is an intentional act of surrender. It says, "God, You are more important to me than food, comfort, convenience, or my daily routines. I want to hear from You, grow closer to You, and depend on You more than anything else."

The goal of fasting is to seek God more intentionally, to realign your heart, and to break through spiritual fog or resistance. When you fast, you deny your body to feed your spirit and to give your full attention to Him.

Fasting helps expose what usually controls your attention or appetite. It quiets the noise of the world and helps you notice what your heart really craves. Without the usual distractions, your spirit becomes more aware of God's presence, and your prayers become more focused and sincere.

Fasting often involves food, but it can also include anything that has taken up too much space in your life: social media, entertainment, noise, busyness, or even certain habits. The goal is not to remove something just for the sake of removal. The goal is to replace it with intentional time in prayer, worship, and Scripture.

When you fast with the right heart, God meets you there. He sharpens your spiritual focus, strengthens your will, and deepens your hunger for His presence. Fasting is not easy, but it is powerful. It reminds your soul that God is your source, not the things you often rely on for comfort or escape.

Fasting is how you say, "Lord, I want more of You.", and God always honors that kind of hunger.

Jesus fasted for 40 days before starting His public ministry (Matthew 4:1-2). Moses fasted before receiving the Ten Commandments (Exodus 34:28). Paul fasted after his conversion (Acts 9:9). The early church fasted before major decisions (Acts 13:2-3). Fasting has always been a key part of preparing, hearing, and obeying.

Here's what's important: You don't fast to impress God. You are not fasting to earn anything from Him. You fast to focus on Him, and in that focus, your spiritual sensitivity increases, your flesh weakens, and your faith strengthens.

Why Fasting Matters for Spiritual Growth

1. **Fasting Breaks the Grip of the Flesh**

    We all have patterns, habits, and impulses that can dominate our lives, often without us realizing it. Fasting quiets the flesh so the spirit can lead. Galatians 5:16 (NIV) says, *"Walk by the Spirit, and you will not gratify the desires of the flesh."* Fasting helps you do exactly that.

2. **Fasting Sharpens Your Spiritual Focus**

When you remove the distraction of food (or media, entertainment, etc.), your attention shifts toward God. You hear His voice more clearly. You recognize distractions more quickly. Your mind slows down, and your heart tunes in.

3. **Fasting Increases Dependence on God**

   When you fast, you quickly realize how much you lean on physical comforts. Fasting pulls you out of autopilot and puts you in a posture of dependence. As you weaken physically, you often grow stronger spiritually.

4. **Fasting Positions You for Breakthrough**

   In Scripture, fasting is often connected to answered prayer, spiritual deliverance, direction, and power. Fasting does not manipulate God, but it aligns your heart with His will. When you get aligned, things begin to move.

How to Fast: Practical Steps for Men

1. **Decide What Type of Fast**

   - **Full Fast:** No food, just water (or liquids like broth/juice).
   - **Partial Fast:** Skipping certain meals or types of food (e.g., a "Daniel fast"–vegetables and water only).
   - **Media/Social Fast:** Abstaining from media or entertainment to reduce distractions and reset focus.

Start small. If you've never fasted before, try one meal, then a day, then work your way up. Let the goal be focus, not intensity.

2. **Set a Purpose for Your Fast**
   - Don't fast without a reason. Set a clear focus: Do you need direction? Freedom? A deeper hunger for God? Clarity on a decision? Write it down and keep it in front of you.

3. **Prepare Your Heart and Schedule**
   - Tell God you're available. Clear space in your schedule for extra time in prayer, Scripture, and stillness. Fasting without prayer is not just abstaining from food. You need both.

4. **Expect Resistance**
   - Your flesh won't like this. You'll feel tired, distracted, and tempted to quit. That's normal. Stay grounded in your original purpose and ask the Holy Spirit for strength.

5. **Break the Fast Gently and Reflect**
   - When it's time to break the fast, don't rush it. Ease back in physically, and more importantly, reflect on what God showed you. What did He reveal? What habits should change? What's next?

When (and Why) to Fast

You don't need a special occasion to fast, but here are moments when fasting is especially helpful:

- You feel spiritually dry or distracted
- You need breakthrough in your battle with sin
- You're seeking clarity for a major decision

- You want to deepen your intimacy with God
- You're preparing for a new season or assignment
- You're interceding for someone or something heavy

Even fasting once a month, or once a quarter, can reset your heart and sharpen your vision.

Let Fasting Become a Regular Weapon

You don't need to fast every week to be spiritual, but you do need moments of deep focus, times when you shut off the noise, quiet your appetite, and get serious about seeking God.

Fasting is an invitation and a reminder that your deepest hunger isn't for food, control, success, or comfort but for the presence of God.

When men fast with purpose, things change. Not always instantly. But over time, walls fall, clarity comes, habits break, and strength grows.

Start where you are, pick a day, choose a fast, set your heart, and trust that God will meet you in the sacrifice.

When men fast with focus, their spiritual lives stop drifting and start advancing.

Chapter 6
The Power of Worship and Praise

Worship Is a Weapon

When most men think of worship, they picture music on a Sunday morning, singing with the congregation, maybe raising a hand or two if they're feeling bold.

Praise and worship are often seen as something for the emotional or the musically inclined, but biblical worship is much more than a song because it's a spiritual weapon. It's a posture of the heart, a declaration of truth, and a key part of walking in spiritual authority.

Psalm 22:3 (NIV) says, *"You are enthroned as the Holy One; You are the one Israel praises."* In other words, God manifests His presence in the praises of His people. Worship is where you draw close to Him, and He draws close to you (James 4:8). It's holy ground.

In Acts 16, Paul and Silas were beaten, imprisoned, and chained in a dungeon, but around midnight, they began to pray and sing hymns to God. Then, what happened? The prison shook. Chains broke. Doors flew open. (Acts 16:25-26). That was the power of praise in action.

Worship is a powerful way to connect with God. As you lift your heart and voice to Him, He meets you with strength, freedom, and clarity.

Worship shifts your focus from the pressure around you to the greatness of God. It quiets fear, lifts discouragement, and fills you with peace and renewed confidence. In worship, you are reminded of who God is and who you are in Him.

In this chapter, we'll break down:

- What worship and praise really are (and why they're different)
- Why they matter to your spiritual growth and strength
- How to cultivate a lifestyle of worship
- How worship reshapes your mind, emotions, and spiritual environment
- How to use praise as a weapon in times of spiritual warfare

To be a man of worship you only need a heart that's surrendered and a life that honors God.

What Are Praise and Worship?

Praise and worship are both vital expressions of your relationship with God. They work together, but they are distinct in purpose and expression.

Praise is how you lift your voice and declare the greatness of God. It is vocal, outward, and full of energy. When you praise, you're proclaiming the truth about who God is and what He has done, His goodness, His power, His faithfulness, and His mercy. Praise builds your faith and breaks through discouragement because it shifts your focus off yourself and onto the character and works of God.

Worship is your personal response to who God is. It's often quieter, more intimate, and centered on the posture of your heart. Worship expresses surrender, love, awe, and reverence. It's how you draw close to God, acknowledging His holiness and giving

Him the honor He deserves. Worship may involve singing, kneeling, silence, prayer, or simply being still in His presence.

The focus here is attitude and attention.

You need both in your life.

- **Praise says:** "God, You are good. You are faithful. You are powerful."
- **Worship says:** "God, I surrender. I'm listening. I honor You."

Praise often opens the door to worship. It gets your eyes off the internal and onto God, and when your perspective shifts, your spirit gets lifted.

As you speak out who God is, your heart begins to soften and respond to Him. This is why so many times in Scripture, you see God's people praising Him with singing, clapping, shouting, and rejoicing before they enter into quiet, reverent worship.

"Enter his gates with thanksgiving and his courts with praise; give thanks to him and praise his name." –Psalm 100:4 (NIV)

You may not feel joyful. You may be tired, stressed, or overwhelmed.

God hasn't changed. He is still worthy, and when you choose to praise and worship anyway, something shifts, not just around you, but within you. God meets you in that place, lifts your spirit, renews your strength, and reminds you that He is present and in control.

You worship because God is worthy. Worship is one of the most powerful ways to stay aligned with God, especially in a world filled with noise, pressure, and distraction. Make it a regular part of your life. It is not a discipline just for Sundays, but every day. Whether through music, silence, prayer, or Scripture, take time to worship. Your soul needs it, and God deserves it.

Here's the key: Worship is who He is. You worship because God is worthy.

Why Worship Matters for a Godly Man

1. **Worship Centers You on Truth**

   - Life throws a lot at you, like stress, temptation, distractions, and demands. Worship anchors you in what's true: God is on the throne, He's in control, and you belong to Him.

2. **Worship Builds Spiritual Strength**

   - Isaiah 40:31 (NIV) says, "Those who hope in the Lord will renew their strength." Worship renews your strength because it reconnects you with the Source. You're reminded that you're not doing life alone or in your own power.

3. **Worship Breaks Spiritual Resistance**

   - There are times when prayer feels heavy and breakthrough feels distant. Worship shifts the atmosphere. It invites God's presence to confront whatever darkness is around you or within you.

4. **Worship Humbles and Aligns Your Heart**

   - A godly man is strong and he's submitted. Worship reminds you that God is God, and you are not. It keeps your pride in check and brings your heart back to the feet of Jesus.

How to Worship Practically (Even If You're Not Musical)

You don't have to be on a worship team to live a life of worship. Here are some practical ways to make praise and worship part of your rhythm:

1. **Start Your Day with Praise**

   - Before you check your phone or scroll through the news, declare something true about God. Say it out loud: "God, You are faithful. You are my strength. I trust You today."

2. **Use Worship Music as a Tool**

   - Build a worship playlist. Use it during your drive, workouts, quiet time, or even while working. Let truth-filled lyrics renew your mind.

3. **Write Out Prayers or Psalms**

   - Expressing worship through written words is powerful. Take a few minutes to write your own psalm or journal your praise to God.

4. **Worship with Your Life**

   - Romans 12:1 (NIV) says, "Offer your bodies as a living sacrifice, holy and pleasing to God—this is your true and proper worship." Worship is how you work, how you treat others, how you honor your wife, how you live with integrity.

Worship in Spiritual Warfare

When you feel spiritually attacked, confused, discouraged, if you're tempted or overwhelmed, don't just struggle with willpower. Instead, worship.

Praise silences the lies of the enemy. It brings your mind under God's truth. It reminds your spirit who's in charge. And it invites the power of God into the middle of your battle.

Psalm 149:6 says, *"May the praise of God be in their mouths and a double-edged sword in their hands."*

That's worship and the Word, together, pushing back the darkness.

Become a Man Who Worships

The enemy fears a man who knows how to worship through the storm. A man who lifts his hands when life is heavy. A man who lifts his voice when fear tries to choke him. A man who bows his heart when pride tries to rise.

That kind of man walks in power. That kind of man stays grounded. That kind of man grows stronger, not just in knowledge, but in relationship with God.

Make worship a part of your daily rhythm. Don't wait for Sunday. Make praise your default setting, make worship your refuge, and watch how your heart, your home, and your spiritual strength begin to shift.

Worship is a deliberate choice, and it leads to freedom, strength, and a deeper intimacy with God.

Chapter 7
Walking in Obedience

Obedience Is the Mark of a Mature Man

Spiritual maturity is reflected in how you respond to God's voice. It shows in your daily choices, especially when obedience requires humility, courage, or sacrifice.

Obedience will not always feel exciting, but it is essential for a strong and growing walk with God. This is where spiritual strength develops and where God's power becomes active in your life. Every grounded and godly man has learned to say yes to God, even when it was difficult, uncomfortable, or came with a personal cost. Obedience is about trusting that God's way is best and following Him one step at a time.

In John 14:15 (NIV), Jesus said, *"If you love me, keep my commands."* Obedience is the evidence of relationship. It's not how we earn God's love; it's how we respond to it. It's love in action.

We live in a culture that celebrates independence, personal freedom, and doing "what feels right." God calls His men to a different standard: obedience that is immediate, humble, and wholehearted. We are not talking about blind obedience. We are talking about faith-filled obedience rooted in trust and the Word.

In this chapter, we'll explore:

- Why obedience is central to spiritual growth
- How to obey even when it's hard, unclear, or risky
- The difference between partial and complete obedience
- The blessings tied to living a life of obedience

- How obedience leads to deeper intimacy and lasting impact

If you want to grow strong, lead well, and walk in God's power, then this is non-negotiable. Obedience is how your faith "gets legs". It's how your convictions get tested, and it's how your life becomes a vessel God can use.

Obedience Starts with Trust

You can't obey someone you don't trust. And you won't trust God if you don't believe He's good.

That's why obedience is about relationship. You obey God when you know He's your Heavenly Father. You obey because you believe that His way is better, even when it doesn't make sense in the moment. His ways are higher than our ways.

Isaiah 55:8-9

"For my thoughts are not your thoughts, neither are your ways my ways," declares the Lord. "As the heavens are higher than the earth, so are my ways higher than your ways and my thoughts than your thoughts.

Proverbs 3:5-6 (NIV) says, *"Trust in the Lord with all your heart and lean not on your own understanding; in all your ways submit to him, and he will make your paths straight."*

The more you trust God, the quicker you'll obey.

The quicker you obey, the more clearly you'll experience His presence and direction in your life.

The Cost of Delayed or Partial Obedience

Delayed obedience is disobedience, as is selective obedience, which is when we obey only the parts of God's Word that are comfortable or convenient.

In 1 Samuel 15, King Saul was told to fully obey God's instructions. He obeyed halfway, kept some things for himself, and justified his actions. But God wasn't impressed. Samuel said, *"To obey is better than sacrifice, and to heed is better than the fat of rams"* (1 Samuel 15:22 NIV).

God doesn't want your excuses. He wants your surrender. When He speaks, He's not asking for negotiation. He's inviting you into alignment.

Obedience in the Everyday

Sometimes obedience means quitting a job or starting a ministry. But more often, it means:

- Confessing sin instead of hiding it
- Apologizing first, even when pride wants to win
- Staying faithful in your marriage
- Tithing when finances feel tight
- Turning off media that pollutes your heart
- Speaking up for truth when it's unpopular
- Serving when you'd rather be served

These decisions shape your character and determine your capacity. If you want to be trusted with more, you have to be faithful with what you already have.

Luke 16:10 (NIV) says, *"Whoever can be trusted with very little can also be trusted with much."*

The Blessing of Obedience

Obedience is a key part of walking closely with God. It opens the way to blessing, clarity, and spiritual authority. When you choose to follow God's direction, you position yourself to experience His favor and guidance in every area of life.

Deuteronomy 28:1-2 (NIV) says, *"If you fully obey the Lord your God and carefully follow all his commands… the Lord your God will set you high above all the nations… All these blessings will come on you and accompany you if you obey the Lord your God."*

Obedience leads to peace, protection, and a sense of purpose. It keeps your heart aligned with God and your life moving in the direction He has prepared for you. As you follow His lead, obedience produces lasting fruit, builds spiritual strength, and draws you into a deeper relationship with Him.

Through obedience, you gain clarity, stability, and courage to walk confidently each day despite inevitable challenges. It becomes a pathway for growth and a steady anchor in every season of life. Obedience opens the door to the life God designed, marked by faith, trust, and lasting impact.

Obedience Is How You Carry the Call

Many men want God to use them in big ways, but few are willing to obey in small, unseen ways. Here's the truth: God prepares you in private before He uses you in public. You can't shortcut that process.

Moses spent 40 years in the wilderness before leading Israel. Joseph endured years in slavery and prison. David served in the fields long before he sat on a throne.

Each of these men was shaped by obedience in the hidden places. When the time came, they were ready. Although they were talented, it was because they were faithful.

A Daily Decision

You won't always feel like obeying, but that's okay, because obedience is about faith, not about feelings. Every day, you have choices:

- Will you do what's easy, or what's right?
- Will you follow culture, or Christ?
- Will you live for comfort, or for calling?

Jesus said in Luke 6:46 (NIV), *"Why do you call me, 'Lord, Lord,' and do not do what I say?"*

That question still stands.

Becoming a Man Who Obeys God

A godly man listens to God's Word and responds with action. He trusts the voice of the One who leads him and chooses to follow with confidence and humility.

When you live with a heart set on obedience, your spiritual life becomes clearer and stronger. Prayer becomes more focused. Your example becomes more credible to those around you. Your daily walk becomes steady and dependable. Obedience creates space for growth, maturity, and spiritual authority.

You are called to walk in step with what God has already shown you. Every step of obedience builds trust, shapes character, and strengthens your foundation. As you follow God's direction, your faith becomes active, and your life begins to reflect the strength and stability that comes from walking closely with Him.

Men who live this way make a difference. They lead their families with integrity, influence others with wisdom, and play a key role in advancing God's Kingdom with purpose and courage.

Start where you are, take the next step, and keep moving forward. God honors a man who walks in obedience.

Part III
Battling for Holiness and Victory

The Fight You Can't Avoid

Every man is in a battle, whether he realizes it or not. The resistance you feel in your spiritual life is not your imagination. There is a real enemy who works to distract your mind, deceive your heart, and drain your strength. He is not a symbol or a vague presence. He is active and intentional.

Ephesians 6:12 (NIV) speaks directly to this reality: *"For our struggle is not against flesh and blood, but against the rulers, against the authorities, against the powers of this dark world and against the spiritual forces of evil in the heavenly realms."*

Your daily challenges may look physical, emotional, or circumstantial, but the true battle is spiritual, and once you recognize it for what it is, you can begin to fight it with the tools God has provided.

The good news is that you are not alone. You are not unequipped. Jesus has already secured victory. He has given you authority, spiritual armor, and His Spirit to live within you. You have everything you need to stand, resist, and walk in victory.

Part 3 discusses preparing for this battle. These chapters will guide you through key areas where many men struggle and where God is calling you to walk in strength:

- **Chapter 8: Spiritual Warfare 101**
    - Learn to recognize the reality of spiritual warfare and how to stand firm using the armor of God.
- **Chapter 9: Overcoming Temptation**
    - Discover how to identify temptation early and respond with strength, truth, and discipline.
- **Chapter 10: Freedom from Strongholds**
    - Break free from the patterns, habits, and lies that have kept you stuck, and walk in lasting freedom.

Regarding these chapters we will discuss fear and freedom ... do not fear but focus on freedom. In spiritual warfare, there is no retreating. Rise up with clarity, courage, and spiritual strength.

Too many men live in quiet defeat simply because they haven't been taught how to fight. That will not be your story. You are called to be alert, equipped, and confident. The battle is real, and so is your victory.

Now is the time to lean in, train well, and walk forward with purpose. You are not stepping into this fight to survive. You are stepping in to overcome.

Chapter 8
Spiritual Warfare 101

Wake Up and Gear Up

Imagine a soldier showing up to the battlefield in gym clothes. No helmet. No weapon. No plan. Just vibes and good intentions.

You wouldn't call that brave. You'd call it foolish, and yet, that's how many men live their spiritual lives. We can find ourselves unaware of the battle, unequipped for the fight, and unarmed against the enemy.

If you want to grow spiritually, lead boldly, and walk in freedom, you can't ignore spiritual warfare.

You need to make sure you do not obsess over demons or see the devil behind every flat tire, but you do need to understand the reality of the battle and how to stand firm in it.

This chapter is your field guide. We'll cover:

- Who the enemy really is and how he works
- What spiritual warfare actually looks like in daily life
- How to recognize schemes and strategies of the enemy
- How to put on and use the armor of God
- How to stand strong
- How to live from victory, not for victory

You do not need to live on the defense. You were called to stand your ground and advance.

Who Is the Enemy?

Satan is active in the world, influencing hearts, minds, and systems with the goal of keeping people bound in sin, fear, confusion, and defeat. This enemy is not a vague sense of darkness or just a symbol of evil.

Scripture clearly identifies Satan as a real spiritual being who opposes God and works to lead people away from truth.

The Bible describes him with specific names and roles:

- The accuser (Revelation 12:10)
- The father of lies (John 8:44)
- The deceiver (2 Corinthians 11:14)
- The tempter (Matthew 4:3)
- A roaring lion looking for someone to devour (1 Peter 5:8)

His tactics often go unnoticed, and appear through subtle lies, distorted truth, quiet compromise, and thoughts that make you question your identity, your worth, or your purpose.

He pushes men toward discouragement and spiritual isolation, while promoting pride, fear, and passivity. His goal is to weaken your walk with God and break your confidence. The truth is that Satan has already been defeated. Jesus claimed victory over him through the cross.

"And having disarmed the powers and authorities, [Jesus] made a public spectacle of them, triumphing over them by the cross." –Colossians 2:15 (NIV)

"I am the Living One; I was dead, and now look, I am alive for ever and ever! And I hold the keys of death and Hades." –Revelation 1:18

Since Jesus has accomplished that victory, it is not yours to fight. You are called to stand in this victory because God has given you the tools to resist the enemy and walk in freedom, clarity, and strength. You have been given spiritual armor, access to truth, and the power of the Holy Spirit to overcome every scheme that comes against you.

Recognizing the Battle in Daily Life

Spiritual warfare often shows up in ordinary moments of everyday life. Rarely does it appear dramatic or obvious. You may face sudden temptation that seems to come out of nowhere. You may struggle with thoughts that quietly repeat lies about your identity, your past, or your worth. Conflict can begin to surface in important relationships, causing tension and emotional distance.

Fear, anxiety, or confusion may settle into your thoughts without a clear reason. You may feel a lingering sense of discouragement or heaviness that weighs you down and steals your motivation. Sometimes, the battle shows up as resistance or distraction when you try to pray, read Scripture, or take a step forward in your spiritual life.

Look out for these and when you begin to see these moments for what they are, your perspective shifts. You become more alert and less likely to fight the wrong battles. Instead of reacting emotionally or giving up, start to respond with prayer, truth, and spiritual focus. The Word of God becomes your weapon. The presence of God becomes your strength. The Spirit of God becomes your guide.

Recognizing the battle is not about fear, but of clarity, and with clarity, you can respond with faith and authority. This awareness is a crucial component of spiritual growth. You are not alone in the fight, and you are not without the tools to stand firm.

How to Recognize Schemes and Strategies of the Enemy

The enemy is subtle. You will find that his strategies often begin with small compromises, quiet lies, or moments of confusion that seem harmless at first. He rarely announces his attack openly. Instead, he works through distraction, deception, division, and discouragement. These patterns can be difficult to identify unless you are spiritually alert and anchored in truth. When you perceive these things happening, you can attribute them to the enemy.

One of the most common strategies is to twist truth just enough to make it sound believable. He plants thoughts that question God's character, distort Scripture, or undermine your identity in Christ.

Remember the serpent in the garden, started with, *"Did God really say ... "* –Genesis 3

These thoughts often echo past failures, feelings of unworthiness, or doubts about whether God really hears your prayers.

Another strategy is to create **division** in your relationships. A simple misunderstanding can grow into bitterness when pride, miscommunication, or unspoken assumptions are left unchecked, and then resentment sets in. The enemy feeds offense and isolation, knowing that disconnection weakens your spiritual life.

Temptation is also a key weapon. It often strikes when you're tired, frustrated, or alone. It promises relief, pleasure, or control, but always leads to guilt, distraction, or bondage. Temptation grows stronger when you keep it hidden or when your guard is down.

Discouragement is another tactic. When prayers go unanswered or spiritual progress feels slow, the enemy will try to convince you that your efforts are pointless. He uses weariness to convince men to settle for survival rather than growth.

Spiritual resistance can also show up when you're trying to take steps forward in faith. You may face unusual challenges, internal pressure, or an unexplainable heaviness. These moments are not random. They often reflect opposition to your growth and calling.

Recognizing these patterns requires spiritual awareness. The more you stay in the Word and connected to God in prayer, the more quickly you will spot what does not align with truth. The Holy Spirit helps you discern what is going on beneath the surface so that you are not caught off guard.

The enemy is real, but he is not creative. His tactics follow familiar patterns. When you understand how he works, you are better prepared to stand strong, resist his influence, and continue moving forward in faith. Staying grounded in truth and consistent in prayer will help you remain clear-headed and spiritually equipped.

The Armor of God (Ephesians 6:10-18)

Paul gives us a clear picture of what we're up against and what God provides:

"Put on the full armor of God, so that you can take your stand against the devil's schemes." –Ephesians 6:11 (NIV)

Here's how to gear up:

1. **Belt of Truth** - Know the truth of God's Word and hold to it. Don't live by feelings. Live by Scripture.

2. **Breastplate of Righteousness** - Walk in obedience and integrity. Righteousness protects your heart from shame and compromise.

3. **Shoes of the Gospel of Peace** - Stay ready to stand and move with peace, knowing your foundation is Christ and your mission is the gospel.

4. **Shield of Faith** - Use your faith to extinguish the lies, doubts, and attacks the enemy throws your way.

5. **Helmet of Salvation** - Guard your mind. Remember who you are in Christ. You're saved, secure, and sealed.

6. **Sword of the Spirit (the Word of God)** - This is your weapon. Speak Scripture. Pray Scripture. Fight lies with truth.

7. **Prayer** - The armor is activated and maintained through prayer. It's not just a piece–it's the power source.

How to Stand Strong

1. **Stay in the Word** - The Bible is your weapon. Read it. Memorize it. Speak it.

2. **Pray daily and consistently** - Don't wait for a crisis. Stay in regular conversation with God.

3. **Live clean** - Confess sin quickly. Don't give the enemy access through compromise.

4. **Stay in community** - You were never meant to fight alone. Isolation is the enemy's playground.

5. **Praise and worship often** - Worship shifts the atmosphere and invites God's presence into your battle.

6. **Take authority in Jesus' name** - You've been given authority over the enemy (Luke 10:19). Use it. Stand in it.

Live From Victory, Not for Victory

You're not fighting *for* victory because Jesus has already won. You're fighting *from* a place of Victory. The enemy can't undo your salvation, but he'll do everything he can to stop your growth, steal your joy, and stall your purpose.

Victory in the Christian life is not something you are trying to earn. It has already been secured through Jesus Christ. His death and resurrection defeated the power of sin, broke the grip of shame, and disarmed the spiritual forces that stand against you. When you place your faith in Him, you are brought into that victory and called to live with confidence and freedom.

Living from victory means standing in what God has already done. It is trusting that His power is at work in your life even when the battle feels intense. It is choosing to respond to challenges from a place of strength, rather than striving to gain something that has already been given.

This mindset changes how you pray, how you respond to temptation, and how you carry yourself as a man of God. You walk with confidence because you know you are already accepted. You resist the enemy because you know he has already been defeated. You remain steady in trials because you know your foundation is secure. You know you are a son.

Victory does not always feel like a rush of emotion or a visible breakthrough. Sometimes it looks like quiet faithfulness, continued obedience, and inner peace in the middle of pressure. It grows as you walk closely with God, stay rooted in His Word, and rely on His Spirit daily.

Jesus never promised that the Christian life would be free of battles, but He did promise that you are not alone and that the outcome is already settled. The more you rest in that truth, the more you live with clarity, purpose, and spiritual strength.

You are not striving to earn worth through performance, success, or spiritual achievements. Your value was established by the One who created you and confirmed by the price Jesus paid to redeem you.

Worth is not measured by victories, titles, or comparison. It is rooted in identity. You belong to the King. You have been chosen, redeemed, and given authority through Christ. You carry His name, His Spirit, and His mission, and because of that, you can live with confidence, stand firm in trials, lead with integrity, and face every battle knowing you are already secure.

This is the kind of confidence that does not come from trying harder. It comes from knowing who you are and walking in the power of what Jesus has already done.

You have what you need:

You have the armor.
You have the Spirit.
You have the Word.
You have the victory.

Now it's time to stand your ground.

Chapter 9
Overcoming Temptation

Winning the Fight Every Man Faces

Every man will encounter temptation. This is a common experience.

Facing temptation is part of life, especially for those who are pursuing a deeper relationship with God, and is not a sign of failure or weakness. It is evidence that you are engaged in a spiritual battle. Even Jesus experienced temptation during His time on earth, as shown in Matthew 4:1-11. His example shows that being tempted means you are walking through the same challenges that every man must face.

Let's be clear: Temptation showing up, in itself, is not sin. Giving in to temptation is.

Too many men feel like failures just for being tempted. The enemy uses that shame to keep them isolated and quiet. The truth is, God provides both the strength to resist and the way out every time.

You will not be able to avoid temptation altogether, but learning how to recognize it, respond to it, and remain grounded in truth is what's key.

A strong man of God learns to rely on Scripture, prayer, and the power of the Holy Spirit when temptation comes. Also, take advantage of spiritual counsel rooted in the word of God.

Growth happens in the moment of choice, when you remember who you are and in whose strength you stand.

Temptation may be persistent, but God provides the wisdom and strength to resist it. You are not alone, and you are not powerless.

James 4:7 says:

Submit yourselves therefore to God. Resist the devil, and he will flee from you.

With every test, there is a way forward, and through every trial, there is a path to greater maturity.

1 Corinthians 10:13 (NIV) says: *"No temptation has overtaken you except what is common to mankind. And God is faithful; He will not let you be tempted beyond what you can bear. But when you are tempted, He will also provide a way out so that you can endure it."*

This chapter is about getting real. We're going to talk plainly about how temptation works, how it hooks you, and how you can break its power as a consistent part of your life.

You can live in freedom. You can develop spiritual reflexes that help you recognize and resist temptation. You can live with a clean conscience, a clear mind, and a strong spirit, but you'll need to be honest, intentional, and equipped.

How Temptation Works

Temptation operates through a deliberate and calculated process aimed at leading you away from your spiritual path and spiritual well-being.

Understanding its mechanics is crucial for effective resistance. James 1:14-15 (NIV) provides insight into this process:

"Each person is tempted when they are dragged away by their own evil desire and enticed. Then, after desire has conceived, it gives birth to sin; and sin, when it is full-grown, gives birth to death."

Recognizing this progression is vital for effectively resisting its pull. This passage outlines a progression that temptation often follows:

1. **Desire**: Temptation often originates from natural human desires or cravings, such as the need for food, rest, or companionship. While these desires are inherently neutral or even positive, they can become problematic when they seek fulfillment outside of appropriate boundaries, which can include being in the form of excess.

2. **Deception**: At this stage, misleading thoughts emerge, portraying the fulfillment of these desires in ways that contradict moral or spiritual principles. The appeal of immediate gratification overshadows potential negative consequences, much like bait concealing a hook from an unsuspecting fish.

3. **Decision**: Here, a choice is made, either to resist the temptation or to succumb to it. This critical moment determines whether one maintains their integrity or steps into actions misaligned with their values.

4. **Disobedience**: Choosing to yield to temptation leads to actions that violate one's ethical or spiritual standards. What began as a natural desire has now manifested as behavior that may cause personal regret or harm to oneself and others.

5. **Death**: The culmination of this process results in adverse outcomes, which may include emotional distress, spiritual disconnection, or other detrimental effects. This underscores the importance of addressing temptation early in its progression.

By understanding and identifying these stages, you can become more vigilant in recognizing the early signs of temptation. This awareness empowers you to interrupt the cycle before it escalates, seeking strength and guidance to uphold your values and commitments.

Common Areas of Temptation for Men

Temptation is a universal challenge that manifests uniquely in each man's life. However, certain areas consistently emerge as significant battlegrounds:

1. Sexual Temptation

Many men grapple with challenges such as pornography, lustful thoughts, fantasies, and inappropriate relationships. In today's digital age, explicit content is readily accessible, as are inappropriate connections and relationships, making it easier to fall into these traps. Engaging in such behaviors can erode self-respect, damage relationships, and create a rift in one's spiritual connection. Recognizing the profound impact of these actions is the first step toward seeking support and establishing boundaries to maintain purity and integrity.

2. Anger and Pride

A quick temper and an inflated ego can lead to strained relationships and poor decision-making. The desire to always be in control or to assert dominance can overshadow humility and patience. Unchecked anger can result in regrettable actions, while pride can prevent personal growth and reconciliation. Cultivating self-awareness and practicing humility can help in managing these emotions effectively.

3. Compromise

The temptation to cut corners, be dishonest, or rationalize unethical behavior often arises in professional and personal settings. Whether it's exaggerating achievements, withholding the truth, or justifying small transgressions, these compromises can accumulate, leading to a compromised character. Upholding honesty and integrity, even when it's challenging, reinforces trustworthiness and self-respect.

4. Addictions

Substances like alcohol and drugs, as well as behaviors like excessive use of social media or overeating, can become addictive. These addictions often serve as coping mechanisms for stress, loneliness, or boredom. They can lead to physical health issues, mental health struggles, and strained relationships. Recognizing the underlying causes and seeking professional help or support groups can be pivotal in overcoming these challenges.

5. Passivity

Neglecting responsibilities, avoiding difficult conversations, or succumbing to spiritual complacency can hinder personal and spiritual growth. Passivity can lead to missed opportunities and unfulfilled potential. Taking proactive steps, setting goals, and embracing challenges can lead to a more fulfilling and purpose-driven life.

The adversary's goal is not necessarily to make you fall in one specific area but to ensnare you in any way possible. Awareness of these common pitfalls equips you to stand guard, seek support, and navigate life's challenges with resilience and faith.

The enemy doesn't care which one gets you stuck as long as he gets you *stuck*.

How to Resist and Overcome Temptation

If willpower alone was the weapon you could use for resisting temptation, that would be difficult enough. You will also need preparation, awareness, and dependence on God's strength. Every man will face temptation, but every man can also learn how to stand strong. God has not left you defenseless. He has given you the tools to fight well and walk in freedom.

Stay Rooted in God's Word

Scripture is your first and most powerful weapon in the battle against temptation. When Jesus faced temptation in the wilderness, He didn't argue or reason with the enemy. He answered with Scripture. Three times He declared, "It is written," and used truth to shut down the lies.

God's Word helps you renew your mind, expose deception, and speak truth into the moment of testing. Keeping Scripture in your heart and on your lips strengthens your spirit and keeps your focus clear.

Here are a few examples of verses to use when temptation strikes:

- When struggling with lust: *"I made a covenant with my eyes not to look lustfully at a young woman."* (Job 31:1)

- When tempted to lie: *"The Lord detests lying lips, but He delights in people who are trustworthy."* (Proverbs 12:22)

- When feeling weak: *"My grace is sufficient for you, for my power is made perfect in weakness."* (2 Corinthians 12:9)

Memorize verses that speak directly to your struggles. Speak them out loud. Let the Word be your sword, not just your safety net.

Pray Before, During, and After the Battle

Prayer keeps you spiritually alert. Before temptation even comes, ask God for wisdom and strength. Build the habit of prayer into your daily rhythm so that when the pressure hits, you are already connected to your source of power.

In the moment of temptation, even a simple prayer matters. You can pray, *"Lord, help me. Strengthen me. I choose You right now."* Prayer realigns your heart, disrupts temptation, and invites God's presence into the moment.

After the moment passes, keep praying whether you resisted or failed. Thank God for victory, or ask for His forgiveness and grace to learn and grow. Prayer keeps your heart soft, humble, and focused on God.

Know Your Triggers and Patterns

Temptation often follows predictable patterns. It shows up when you're hungry, angry, lonely, or tired, known by the acronym HALT. Pay attention to what makes you vulnerable. Is it isolation? Stress? Late nights online? Unfiltered access to certain apps or websites?

Knowing your personal triggers does not make you weak. It makes you wise. When you identify the times and conditions that open the door to temptation, you can prepare for them, limit your exposure, or choose a different response.

Have a Clear Exit Plan

When temptation shows up, the time to decide your response has already passed. If you wait until the moment to come up with a strategy, you are far more likely to fall. Having a plan ahead of time gives you a path out.

Make the decision now about what you will do. Step away from the situation. Block the app or website. Install accountability software. Call a friend. Get out of the room. Shut the screen. Walk outside. Do something that breaks the cycle immediately.

God always provides a way of escape. Your responsibility is to take it quickly and decisively.

Walk with Brothers, Not Alone

Every man needs a circle of brothers who are walking in the same direction. These are the men who can ask hard questions, speak truth in love, pray with you, and help you get back up when you fall. You were not created to fight these battles alone.

Isolation is dangerous because it allows shame and secrecy to grow. Temptation thrives in the dark, but when you open up to a trusted brother in Christ, the power of shame starts to lose its grip.

Ecclesiastes 4:9-10 (NIV) reminds us, *"Two are better than one… If either of them falls down, one can help the other up."*

Freedom grows when you walk in honesty, accountability, and encouragement with other men who are committed to the same pursuit of godliness.

Temptation is real, but so is the strength God provides. You are not powerless, you are not alone, and you are not stuck. Through God's Word, prayer, awareness, and the support of others, you can resist temptation and grow stronger every time.

When You Fall, Get Back Up Quickly

Every man faces moments of failure. You may give in to temptation or make a decision you regret. When that happens, the most important step is to return to God without delay. Failure is not the end of the story. It becomes a turning point when you respond with humility and honesty.

1 John 1:9 (NIV) offers a powerful promise: *If we confess our sins, He is faithful and just and will forgive us our sins and purify us from all unrighteousness."*

When you confess your sin, God responds with forgiveness, cleansing, and restoration. Confession opens the door. Repentance shifts your direction. Grace lifts the burden. Grace is not withheld from you.

Guilt tries to convince you to hide, delay, or disconnect, but grace invites you to return, be restored, and keep growing. The sooner you come back to God, the sooner healing begins. There is no need to carry shame longer than it takes to bring it into the light.

When you fall, get up, reset your focus, and turn your heart back to truth. Let God strengthen what was weak and continue the work He started in you.

Living a Lifestyle of Purity and Strength

Victory over temptation comes through daily dependence on the presence and power of the Holy Spirit, and not with gritted teeth or relying on human effort.

Galatians 5:16 (NIV) gives the foundation: *"So I say, walk by the Spirit, and you will not gratify the desires of the flesh."*

Walking by the Spirit is a daily choice. It happens as you spend time with God, open His Word, listen for His voice, and yield to His direction. The more you stay connected to Him, the more your heart is transformed. Your desires begin to change, your perspective becomes clearer, and your convictions grow stronger.

A life of purity is built in thousands of small decisions, shaped by the Spirit of God working within you. It takes time, consistency, and grace. You are being formed into someone who no longer craves what once held you back.

Freedom is pursuing intimacy with Jesus and is also resisting sin. The more you say yes to Him, the less space temptation has to work in your life.

You Can Win the Fight

Temptation will come. It may hit hard, and it may come often, but the power of the Holy Spirit is stronger. You have been given everything you need to stand firm, respond wisely, and grow stronger.

You are a man of God. You are forgiven. You are filled with the Spirit. You are not without help. You are not without direction. You are not stuck.

You are learning to walk in wisdom, strength, and victory, one day, one step, one decision at a time.

Stay focused, make a plan, remain alert, and keep your heart soft and your hands clean. Walk closely with God and keep moving forward.

Victory is seen in a man who keeps getting up, keeps choosing truth, and refuses to live in defeat. That is the life of a godly man. That is the life God has called you to live, and by His grace, it is the life you will walk in.

Chapter 10
Freedom from Strongholds

You Don't Have to Stay Stuck

In the journey of faith, believers encounter various challenges. Some are brief and swiftly overcome, while others persist, testing endurance and resolve. These enduring struggles often signal the presence of spiritual strongholds.

A stronghold represents a deeply rooted pattern of thinking, behavior, or response that influences one's life.

These are more than mere habits; they are areas where repeated experiences, choices, or deceptions have allowed entrenched patterns to form.

Devoted believers, sincere in their faith journey, may still find themselves confronting issues such as anger, lust, insecurity, addiction, fear, shame, or pride. Although the desire for change exists, these challenges persist, and they often stem from deeper, unaddressed areas within.

The encouraging truth is that God's plan encompasses not only forgiveness but also complete liberation. Believers are invited to release burdens that have already been lifted through Christ's sacrifice and to step into the freedom that has been assured.

As stated in 2 Corinthians 10:3-5 (NIV): *"For though we live in the world, we do not wage war as the world does. The weapons we fight with... have divine power to demolish strongholds. We demolish arguments and every pretension that sets itself up against the knowledge of God..."*

This chapter aims to equip you with effective strategies for this spiritual battle. You will gain insights into identifying strongholds and learn methods to dismantle them through truth, repentance, spiritual authority, and consistent action.

The journey to freedom is a transformative process, and pursuing it leads to a life of greater purpose and power.

What Is a Stronghold?

Understanding Spiritual Strongholds

A spiritual stronghold is a deeply entrenched pattern of thinking or behavior that stands in opposition to God's truth. These strongholds act as fortified positions within our minds, influencing our perceptions, decisions, and interactions. They often develop over time, rooted in deception and sustained by various negative experiences or choices.

Recognizing the Voice of a Stronghold

A spiritual stronghold often shows itself through repeated thoughts or beliefs that compete with what God says about your identity and future. These are not passing ideas but deeply rooted patterns that influence how you think, feel, and live.

Strongholds can sound like inner voices whispering thoughts such as:
"I will never overcome this struggle."
"I am not enough for what God is calling me to do."
"This is just the way I am, and nothing will change it."
"God probably uses others, but not someone like me."
"People cannot be trusted, so it is safer to stay distant."
"If I forgive, I am letting them off the hook."
"My worth is determined by my achievements."

"Showing emotions is a sign of weakness."
"I cannot ask for help; I have to handle this alone."

These statements reveal underlying beliefs that can create barriers between you and the abundant life God intends. They may stem from past experiences, cultural influences, or misunderstandings of God's character.

Instead of seeing life through the lens of God's promises, your vision becomes clouded by old lies and fears. Over time, these thoughts can influence your confidence, your relationships, your choices, and even how you respond to God.

Recognizing these patterns is a powerful first step towards transformation. When you see them for what they are, you can open the door to replacing them with the liberating truths found in Scripture and the knowledge of who God says you are: chosen, loved, redeemed, and empowered to live in freedom.

Origins of Strongholds

Several factors can contribute to the formation of strongholds:

- **Repeated Sin**: Engaging in habitual sins, such as sexual immorality, substance abuse, or deceit, can create neural pathways that make these behaviors feel inescapable.

- **Trauma or Abuse**: Unhealed wounds from past traumatic experiences can lead to protective but unhealthy thought patterns, such as distrust or feelings of unworthiness.

- **Generational Patterns**: Behaviors or beliefs passed down through family lines can establish cycles that seem normal but are contrary to God's design.

- **Unforgiveness**: Harboring resentment towards others or oneself can solidify bitterness, negatively impacting one's emotional and spiritual well-being.

- **Shame**: Internalizing guilt or embarrassment, especially when concealed, can distort one's self-image and hinder openness to God's grace.

Over time, these elements intertwine, influencing how we view ourselves, relate to others, and perceive God. They can lead to a sense of bondage, where individuals feel trapped, ashamed, frustrated, powerless, and ultimately defeated.

The Path to Freedom

Despite the seeming strength of these strongholds, they are vulnerable to the transformative power of God's truth. Recognizing and confronting these lies with Scripture and prayer can dismantle their influence.

Engaging in community with other believers provides support and accountability. Seeking professional counseling or pastoral guidance can also be instrumental in addressing deep-seated issues. We will discuss this in detail as we continue through these pages.

Remember, no stronghold is beyond the reach of God's grace. By identifying these fortified lies and actively replacing them with divine truth, you can experience the freedom and renewal that comes from aligning your mind and heart with God's perspective.

Identifying a Stronghold in Your Life

Now that you have learned what a stronghold is and the patterns, identifying spiritual strongholds in your life is a crucial step toward experiencing the freedom and transformation that God desires for you.

Remember, a **spiritual stronghold** is a deeply entrenched pattern of thinking or behavior that opposes the knowledge and truth of God, which manifests as habitual sins, persistent negative thoughts, or emotional wounds that seem resistant to change.

Signs You May Be Dealing with a Stronghold

- **Recurring Sin Patterns:** Despite your sincere efforts and prayers, you find yourself repeatedly falling into the same sinful behaviors, such as engaging in pornography, substance abuse, or dishonesty.

- **Feelings of Powerlessness:** There are areas in your life where you feel out of control, leading to frustration and a sense of defeat.

- **Distorted Self-Perception:** You struggle with feelings of unworthiness, believing you're unloved or disqualified from God's grace, even when Scripture affirms otherwise.

- **Dominance of Internal Lies:** Negative thoughts and lies about yourself or God are louder and more convincing than His truth, leading to doubt and confusion.

- **Sabotaging Relationships and Spiritual Growth:** You might avoid deepening relationships or spiritual commitments due to fear, mistrust, or feelings of inadequacy.

- **Emotional Discrepancies:** Experiencing emotions like numbness or intense anger that seem disproportionate to the situation can indicate underlying strongholds.

Reflective Action

Take a moment to seek God's insight into your life.

Pray this short prayer with an open heart:

"Lord, are there any strongholds in my life that I've accepted as normal?"

Or, as an expanded prayer, pray this, again with an open heart:

Father, I come before You with humility and a desire to walk in the freedom You have promised. Thank You for loving me completely and for desiring truth and healing in every part of my life. I invite You to search my heart and reveal anything that does not align with Your Word. Show me any strongholds I have allowed to take root, whether through past wounds, lies I have believed, or patterns I have accepted as normal.

I ask You to bring to light any hidden areas that keep me bound. Help me to see clearly where the enemy has tried to build walls of fear, shame, pride, addiction, or insecurity. As You reveal these areas, fill me with courage to confront them with Your truth.

I reject every lie that does not come from You. I choose to believe what You say about me. I trust that Your power is greater than any struggle or stronghold. By the authority of Jesus Christ, I ask You to begin the work of tearing down every false belief and breaking every chain that holds me back.

Lead me in repentance, renew my mind, and restore my heart. Strengthen me by Your Spirit to walk in freedom, victory, and purpose. I belong to You, and I will stand on Your promises. Thank You for never giving up on me. I am ready to move forward in Your strength.

In the name of Jesus, Amen.

Be still and listen. God desires to reveal these areas, not to bring condemnation, but to lead you toward healing and freedom. As He brings strongholds to light, trust in His grace, trust in His power, and be willing to walk with others who can support you on this journey.

Remember, acknowledging the presence of a stronghold is the first step toward breaking free from its grip. With God's guidance, the support of a faith community, and possibly professional counseling, you can begin the journey toward renewed thinking and living in the fullness of God's truth.

How to Tear Down a Stronghold and Walk in Deliverance

1. Expose the Lie

The enemy's power lies in deception. Once the lie is exposed, it begins to lose its grip.

Ask yourself:

- What thought patterns do I keep repeating that contradict God's Word?
- What lies have I believed about myself, God, or others?

Then bring those lies into the light.

Example:

- Lie: *"I'll never be free from porn."*
  Truth: *"It is for freedom that Christ has set me free."* (Galatians 5:1)
- Lie: *"I'm broken beyond repair."*
  Truth: *"If anyone is in Christ, he is a new creation."* (2 Corinthians 5:17)

2. Repent and Renounce

Once each lie is exposed, take authority.

Repentance is more than feeling sorry. It's turning away from agreement with the enemy and aligning with God.

Pray:

"Lord, I repent for believing [name the lie]. I renounce the enemy's hold in this area. I break agreement with it in Jesus' name."

You have spiritual authority so use it. Luke 10:19: *I have given you authority to trample on snakes and scorpions and to overcome all the power of the enemy; nothing will harm you.*

3. Replace the Lie with Truth

Strongholds can be removed, but they must also be replaced with truth. Begin to declare what God's Word says daily, out loud, and with conviction. You're renewing your mind (Romans 12:2).

Write down Scriptures that speak to the area you're targeting. Say them in prayer. Post them where you'll see them. Use them in moments of temptation or fear.

4. Invite Accountability and Prayer

Don't fight strongholds alone. Confess to a trusted brother in Christ. Ask for prayer. Invite someone to check in on you.

James 5:16 (NIV): *"Confess your sins to each other and pray for each other so that you may be healed."*

Freedom is a community project.

5. Stay Persistent

Strongholds often take time to dismantle fully. It's not one-and-done. But every time you resist the lie, speak truth, and walk in obedience, another brick comes down.

Freedom grows with consistency. The more you walk in the Spirit, the weaker the flesh becomes.

What Freedom Feels Like

When strongholds fall, you'll start to notice:

- Mental clarity where there was confusion
- Peace where there was anxiety
- Hope where there was despair
- Spiritual authority where there was fear
- A clean conscience and renewed confidence in God

You'll walk lighter. Pray bolder. Lead better. Love more freely.

Because freedom isn't just about avoiding sin—it's about becoming who God made you to be.

Jesus Came to Set You Free

Luke 4:18 (NIV) says: *"He has sent me to proclaim freedom for the prisoners… to set the oppressed free."*

That mission is a forever mission and didn't end in the Gospels. It's still true for you. Jesus didn't save you so you could limp through life in quiet bondage. He saved you to live free, love well, and walk in His power.

Strongholds don't fall by accident. But they *do* fall when godly men take authority, apply truth, and stay in the fight.

You don't have to stay stuck. You can be free and your freedom will become a testimony that strengthens others.

Part IV
Leading and Impacting with Power

Introduction: Your Leadership Matters More Than You Think

You are leading someone even if you don't realize it.

It might be your wife, your children, your coworkers, your friends, your church, or even the people watching how you live when you don't think anyone is paying attention.

Leadership may include position but it is primarily about influence, and every man of God is called to lead.

The problem is, most men feel unqualified. They think spiritual leadership is for pastors, elders, or guys who have it all figured out. But God's Word tells a different story.

From Genesis to Revelation, God consistently calls ordinary men, often flawed and fearful, to lead in extraordinary ways through His strength.

You were created to lead, not control.

To serve, not dominate. To influence, not impress.

Spiritual leadership is about being the most surrendered.

Part 4 will equip you to lead the way Jesus led: with courage, humility, conviction, and sacrificial love. Whether you're leading a family, a team, a ministry, or simply through the example of your life, God wants to use your leadership to shape others and point them toward Him.

This section is about becoming a faithful steward of the influence God has entrusted to you.

We begin with the foundation: understanding the role of a spiritual leader.

Chapter 11
The Role of a Spiritual Leader

Leadership Begins with Surrender

Many men chase leadership for status or control. But biblical leadership begins in a completely different place: surrender to God.

Leadership is an integral part of life, influencing our families, workplaces, communities, and personal growth. Among various forms of leadership, spiritual leadership holds a distinctive and profound role. It transcends mere guidance by inspiring others to align with a higher purpose and deeper meaning.

It is a calling that extends to anyone willing to guide others toward truth, integrity, and fulfillment. This form of leadership emphasizes service over authority, focusing on uplifting others and fostering environments where individuals can thrive spiritually and morally.

Before you can lead others well, you have to be led by Him. Before you can offer direction, you need to walk in submission. The strength of your leadership depends entirely on the strength of your connection to Christ.

Jesus modeled this perfectly. Though He had all authority, He served others, washed feet, prayed in secret, and submitted to the Father in everything—even unto death.

In Luke 22:26 (NIV), Jesus said, *"The greatest among you should be like the youngest, and the one who rules like the one who serves."*

Leadership in the Kingdom is upside down. It's not about being in charge. It's about taking responsibility, walking in integrity, and laying your life down for those you lead.

This chapter will help you:

- Understand what biblical leadership looks like
- Identify where and how you're already leading
- Embrace your role as a servant-leader in your home, church, and community
- Develop habits that strengthen your leadership
- Avoid common pitfalls that derail godly influence

Whether you feel ready or not, God has called you to lead. And He equips those He calls.

What Is Spiritual Leadership?

Spiritual leadership begins with personal submission to God. True leadership flows from a life that is aligned with God's heart and committed to His purposes. A spiritual leader influences others by the way he lives, speaks, serves, and sacrifices.

Spiritual leadership is seen most clearly in daily actions, often long before it is recognized with any formal role. It is rooted in consistency, humility, and a desire to point others to Christ. A spiritual leader is someone who follows Jesus not only in public but also in private. His faithfulness in the small things creates a foundation of trust and strength that others can follow.

A man who leads spiritually lives with integrity. His character remains steady even when no one is watching. He speaks truth in love, protects those entrusted to his care, and nurtures their spiritual well-being. He takes responsibility for the people, opportunities, and influence that God has placed in his hands. His leadership style is marked by service rather than control, by courage rather than passivity, and by humility rather than pride.

Spiritual leaders are called to be faithful, not expected to be flawless. They repent quickly when they fall short. They listen carefully to God and to the people around them. They love with depth and strength. Their lives act as a signpost, consistently pointing others back to the grace, truth, and power of Christ.

Spiritual leadership is can often be seen and expected to be for a select few, but it is not. It is the calling of every man who has chosen to follow Jesus.

In every home, church, workplace, and relationship, God is raising up men who will lead with a heart fully surrendered to Him.

Remember, a spiritual leader, in short, is someone who:

- Follows Jesus consistently
- Lives with integrity, even when no one is watching
- Protects and nurtures the spiritual health of others
- Takes responsibility for what God has entrusted to him
- Serves first, speaks truth, and leads with courage and humility

Spiritual leaders are faithful, repent quickly, listen well, and love deeply.

Where You're Called to Lead

Spiritual leadership extends into every aspect of life, calling men to guide with faith and integrity in various environments. This leadership is not confined to formal roles within a church but is demonstrated through daily actions and decisions.

Leading In Your Home

Your home is the first and most important place where God has called you to lead. This is where your influence is most consistent and most powerful.

Leadership at home is more than just setting up a family devotion time or ensuring everyone prays before meals. Those are good, but real leadership shows up in how you live every day.

When you show love, patience, and humility in your home, you are teaching your family what faith looks like in real life. Every moment of kindness, every time you ask for forgiveness when you get it wrong, every decision you make to put others first is shaping your family's understanding of who God is.

If you're a father, you are responsible for leading your children in truth, discipline, and love (Deuteronomy 6:6-7; Ephesians 6:4), because they need presence, consistency, and example.

If you're single, you still lead. Your choices now shape your future influence. You lead through your lifestyle, your words, and your example in relationships, work, and ministry.

Talk about faith openly. Make it normal to bring up questions about God, Scripture, and prayer around the dinner table, in the car, or during everyday conversations.

Do not get caught up in needing to have all the answers. What matters is that you create an environment where faith is part of the real, living fabric of your family life.

When you lead this way, you build a home where each person feels valued, heard, and loved. You are protecting your family and you are nurturing their spiritual foundation.

You are helping them see that following Jesus is not a performance; it is a way of life.

Leading in Your Church

Your church needs you. Spiritual leadership inside the church is not about waiting for someone to give you a title. It starts with showing up with a heart ready to serve.

Look for ways to get involved. You might lead a small group, mentor a younger believer, or use your skills to strengthen a ministry team.

When you step up to serve, you send a powerful message that the church is not just a place you attend, but a family you help build. Your willingness to invest time, energy, and encouragement helps others grow stronger in their faith.

Leadership in the church creates a culture of service and support. When you serve, you inspire others to step forward and use their gifts too. You help create an environment where people feel loved, equipped, and sent out to make a difference. That is the heartbeat of a thriving spiritual family.

Leading in Your Workplace

God has placed you in your workplace on purpose. Your job is not just about earning a paycheck. It is also a place where your faith can shine. Spiritual leadership at work looks like treating people with integrity, fairness, and respect. It shows up when you honor your word, go the extra mile, and handle challenges with grace and wisdom.

You may not always be able to discuss your faith openly at work, but your life will speak for itself. The way you work, the way you treat people, and the way you handle pressure can open doors for conversations and influence.

A man who leads well in the workplace helps build an environment of trust, excellence, and compassion. He stands out because his actions reflect the character of Christ, even without needing to say a word.

Leading in Daily Life

Spiritual leadership does not stop when you leave work or church. It weaves through every part of your daily life. You have opportunities every day to lead by example with your neighbors, in your community, while driving on the road, and with the people you encounter in everyday moments, such as while shopping, and patronizing local restaurants and coffee shops.

Simple acts of kindness, standing up for what is right, and offering help when someone needs it all matter. Every choice to live out your faith in public gives others a glimpse of who Jesus is. Your consistency builds influence that goes far beyond the people you know personally.

When you stay faithful in the small things, God uses your life to stir something greater in the world around you. Leadership in daily life may not always feel big or dramatic, but it is powerful because it is real and steady, and you may never know the impact on others.

The Call to Lead Everywhere You Go

Spiritual leadership is a commitment to personal growth and serving others effectively. It is a way of living that touches every sphere you step into. When you live this way, you not only strengthen your own spiritual journey, but you also help build up the people around you.

God has called you to be a leader wherever you are. When you lead with a heart surrendered to Him, your influence carries weight that reaches far beyond what you can see.

You lead by how you carry yourself. Your integrity, attitude, work ethic, and treatment of others all point somewhere. Are they pointing people to Christ?

How to Lead with Strength and Integrity

Leading with strength and integrity is not about being perfect. It is about being faithful, intentional, and consistent across every part of your life. Your home, your church, your workplace, and your community all need the influence of a man who leads well. Here are six keys to help you lead with strength and integrity.

Abide in Christ Daily

You cannot lead well if you are spiritually empty. Staying connected to Christ is the foundation of all real leadership. Spend time in God's Word every day. Pray with honesty and expectation. Keep your heart soft and your ears open to His voice. When you stay rooted in Christ, you have the strength to give. Your leadership flows out of the relationship you cultivate with Him, not out of your own efforts.

Own Your Responsibility

Leadership can be something you wait to be invited into, but God has already called you to lead right where you are. Step into it with confidence. Lead in your home by setting the spiritual tone and loving your family well. Lead in your church by showing up and serving where there is a need. Lead in your workplace by working with excellence and integrity. Leadership starts by seeing what needs to be done and moving toward it with a willing heart.

Practice What You Preach

Integrity is the anchor of spiritual leadership. The man who leads well lives the same way when no one is watching as he does when everyone is looking. Your example will always speak louder than your words. When you are consistent in how you live, trust grows. Your family, your coworkers, and your community will follow a man who lives out the truth with authenticity and courage.

Serve First, Speak Second

Jesus showed us the way. He served before He spoke. He put the needs of others before His own. Leadership is not about controlling people. It is about loving and serving them. You lead best when you lay down pride and choose humility. Look for opportunities to serve your family, your church, your neighbors, and even those with whom you disagree. When you serve first, your words carry weight, and your leadership leaves a mark that matters.

Commit to Continuous Growth

Every great leader remains a lifelong learner. Growth never stops, no matter how long you have been walking with God. Stay humble enough to recognize where you need to grow. Ask for feedback from those closest to you. Be willing to hear it without defensiveness. Invite your wife, your kids, your pastor, or a trusted friend to speak into your life. Surround yourself with men who sharpen you and challenge you. Leadership requires courage to keep growing when it would be easier to stay comfortable. When you commit to growth, you will lead with more wisdom, patience, and strength everywhere you go.

Ask for Feedback and Correction

A man who wants to lead well knows he cannot see everything clearly on his own. Regularly seek out honest feedback. Ask the people who know you best, "How can I grow as a spiritual leader?" Listen carefully. Thank them for their honesty. Let their insights sharpen you.

A teachable spirit not only strengthens your leadership but also models humility and grace for those watching your life.

Pitfalls That Undermine Leadership

Leading with strength and integrity is a high calling, but leadership without vigilance can slowly drift off course. Being aware of the common pitfalls helps you stay grounded, faithful, and effective in every place God has called you to lead.

Neglecting Personal Spiritual Health

Your leadership will only be as strong as your personal walk with God. When you neglect your time in prayer, Scripture, and worship, your heart slowly grows tired and your influence weakens.

Staying rooted in Christ keeps you fresh, humble, and full of life. Your personal spiritual health is not a luxury; it is a necessity.

Passivity

One of the oldest traps is passivity. Adam's failure in the Garden was not that he did something wrong, but that he stayed silent when he should have stepped up. Leadership requires movement. Avoiding responsibility, remaining silent when you should speak, and shrinking back when your voice is needed will rob you of the impact you are meant to have. Step forward, even when it feels uncomfortable.

Pride

Pride quietly kills leadership. It convinces you that leadership is about control, about being the smartest man in the room, or about being noticed and honored. Pride isolates a leader from the people he is called to serve and eventually crumbles everything built on it. True leadership flows from humility. God opposes the proud but gives grace to the humble. Stay low. Stay teachable. Stay focused on serving rather than shining.

Compromise

Nothing erodes leadership faster than hidden sin or moral compromise. When you live one way in public and another way in private, your authority drains out. Trust begins to crack. Compromise in small areas always leads to bigger falls if left unchecked. Pursue holiness. Protect your integrity. Be the same man behind closed doors that you are when everyone is watching.

Avoiding Difficult Conversations

Spiritual leaders do not shy away from difficult conversations. Whether it is in your home, workplace, or church, issues do not resolve themselves with silence. Avoiding them only allows problems to grow roots. Approach difficult conversations with grace, truth, and a heart to restore, not to wound. Being willing to have hard conversations shows courage and care for the people you are called to lead.

Resisting Feedback

A strong leader has a soft heart toward correction. If you dismiss feedback or defend yourself every time someone points something out, growth stops.

Great leaders stay teachable. Invite feedback. Thank the people who are willing to tell you the truth. Correction is a gift when you see it through the lens of growth.

Overextending Commitments

Taking on too much can wear you down and make you less effective in all aspects of life. It can also cause your most important leadership areas, like your family, to suffer. Know your limits. Learn to say yes to the right things and no to distractions. Margin in your life makes you stronger, not weaker.

Isolating Yourself

Leadership can sometimes feel lonely, but choosing isolation only makes it harder. Lone wolves do not lead well for long. Isolation cuts you off from support, correction, and encouragement. Surround yourself with other godly men who sharpen you, encourage you, and challenge you to stay faithful. Iron sharpens iron, and you were not meant to lead alone.

You Were Made to Lead

Leadership isn't for a select few; it's part of your design. God created men to carry spiritual responsibility, not as a burden, but as a **blessing** and a **mission**.

The world needs more men who lead with character. The Church needs more men who lead with courage. Families need more men who lead with love. And God is calling you–not someday, but now.

You don't need to have it all figured out. You just need to show up with a surrendered heart, a willing spirit, and the conviction to keep growing.

Godly men don't wait for a platform to lead. They lead where they are, with what they've been given, for the glory of the One who called them.

Chapter 12
Discipleship and Brotherhood

You Weren't Meant to Grow Alone

You can't become the man God called you to be on your own. Period.

Spiritual growth is not a solo project. You were created for relationship, not isolation. From the very beginning, God made it clear when He said, "It is not good for the man to be alone" (Genesis 2:18 NIV). That truth reaches far beyond marriage. It speaks to every part of life, especially your spiritual journey.

God designed growth to happen within community. You are meant to walk alongside others. You are not designed to struggle by yourself. You need deep, honest, Spirit-filled brotherhood and not just surface-level friendships. You need men who know you, challenge you, encourage you, sharpen you, and hold you accountable.

Discipleship and brotherhood are not optional for men who want to live strong, faithful lives. They are essential. You will never become the man God designed you to be without the influence of other godly men around you.

Look at how Jesus led His disciples. He did not set up a classroom. He did life with them. He walked dusty roads with them. He shared meals, corrected mistakes, prayed over them, spoke truth into their confusion, and sent them out to change the world. He built a brotherhood that carried the gospel to the ends of the earth.

You are called to live the same way. You need other men who will walk beside you. And other men need you to walk beside them. Discipleship and brotherhood are not reserved for the spiritually elite. They are a normal and necessary part of a strong, healthy spiritual life.

In this chapter, we will dig into what this looks like in real life. We will cover:

- What true biblical discipleship looks like and how it works
- Why brotherhood is vital for long-term spiritual strength
- How to pursue and build strong, godly friendships
- How to disciple others even when you feel unsure or unqualified
- How to recognize and resist isolation, one of the enemy's most effective traps against men

If you want to grow strong and stay strong, you must walk with men who are heading in the same direction. Brotherhood is not a luxury. It is a calling and a lifeline.

What Is Discipleship?

Discipleship is about intentionally following Jesus, learning from Him, and striving to reflect His character in every aspect of your life. In addition to acquiring knowledge, you seek transformation through a deep, personal commitment to His teachings and mission. This journey flourishes within a community of believers.

Consider how Jesus discipled others. He invited individuals into close fellowship, sharing daily life with them. Through these interactions, He demonstrated how to live in alignment with God's will, showing compassion, humility, and unwavering faith.

His disciples didn't just hear His words; they observed His actions and were transformed by His example.

This relational approach reveals that discipleship is more than academic learning; it's about life transformation through connection with Christ and fellow believers.

True discipleship also involves obedience to Jesus' commands and active participation in His mission. In the Great Commission (Matthew 28:19-20), Jesus instructs us to make disciples of all nations, baptizing them and teaching them to observe all He has commanded. This means discipleship is both about being a disciple and making disciples.

As you grow in your relationship with Christ, you're called to invest in others, guiding and encouraging them in their spiritual journey.

Moreover, discipleship requires a willingness to prioritize Jesus above all else. In Luke 14:26-27, Jesus emphasizes that following Him may demand significant sacrifices, including reordering our personal priorities and commitments. This level of devotion reflects the seriousness of true discipleship and the depth of commitment required to walk in His footsteps.

In essence, biblical discipleship is a holistic, transformative process.

It's about learning from Jesus, living in community with other believers, obeying His teachings, participating in His mission, and committing wholeheartedly to His path.

It's a lifelong journey of becoming more like Christ and helping others do the same.

Jesus gave a clear mission in Matthew 28:19-20 (NIV): *"Go and make disciples of all nations… teaching them to obey everything I have commanded you."*

This is more than a church role. It's a man's calling.

Discipleship starts with your willingness to:
- Walk with someone consistently
- Be honest about your own journey
- Open God's Word together
- Encourage, challenge, and pray for each other
- Model what it looks like to follow Christ

Discipleship is more caught than taught. Your life is the message. Your consistency is the curriculum.

What Is Brotherhood?

Brotherhood is much more than having a few friends. Brotherhood is a circle of men who are committed to sharpening one another, speaking truth with love, and walking through the ups and downs of life side by side.

Think about Proverbs 27:17, which says, *"As iron sharpens iron, so one person sharpens another."* You have probably seen this as a nice phrase to put on a coffee mug or a t-shirt, but it is a spiritual necessity if you want to grow strong and stay sharp in your walk with God.

When you have real brotherhood, you are surrounded by men who know how to encourage you when life weighs heavily.

They will step in and hold you up when your strength feels low. They will pray for you when you cannot seem to find the words to pray for yourself. They will celebrate the victories God gives you and remind you to keep giving Him the glory.

Brotherhood also means having men in your life who love you enough to correct you when you start drifting. They are not there to shame you or control you. They are there to call you back to who God has made you to be. Their love and truth will inspire you to keep growing, rather than settling for less.

You do not need a dozen brothers. You need a few faithful ones. You need men with whom you can be completely honest, men who will not flinch when you confess your struggles, and men who will not let you give up when the road gets tough.

This kind of brotherhood does not happen by accident. It takes intentionality, humility, and time. But when you find it, it becomes one of the greatest sources of strength, growth, and encouragement you will ever experience.

In brotherhood, you have:

- **Encouragement** when life gets hard
- **Accountability** when sin creeps in
- **Prayer** when you don't have strength
- **Celebration** when you win
- **Correction** when you drift

You don't need a dozen brothers, but you do need a few men you can be completely honest with and men who won't flinch at your failures and won't let you settle for less than what God has for you.

How to Pursue Brotherhood and Discipleship

Simply. Humbly. Effectively.

Cultivating godly friendships is vital for your spiritual growth and well-being. These relationships provide support, encouragement, and accountability as you navigate life's journey. Building such friendships requires intentional effort and a heart aligned with Christ's teachings.

Pray for Meaningful Connections

Begin by seeking God's guidance in forming friendships. Ask Him to bring individuals into your life who will uplift and challenge you in your faith. Trust that He knows your needs and will provide companions who share your commitment to spiritual growth.

Engage in Community Activities

Participate actively in your church and local community. Join small groups, Bible studies, or service projects where you can meet like-minded individuals. Serving alongside others fosters bonds rooted in shared faith and purpose. As you work together, you'll find opportunities to build and deepen friendships.

Don't wait for someone else to take the lead. Reach out.

Say:

"I've been thinking about growing more intentionally in my faith. Would you want to grab coffee sometime and talk about it?"

Prioritize Time Together and Meet Regularly with Purpose

Schedule regular meetings, whether for prayer, study, or simply enjoying each other's company. Invest time. Consistency strengthens relationships and demonstrates your commitment to the process and to one another.

Start with once a week or every other week. Open the Word. Talk about real life. Pray together. Keep it intentional and not just social.

Ask questions like:

- What is God teaching you right now?
- Where are you struggling?
- What do you need prayer for?
- What's one step of obedience you're working on?

Be Open and Vulnerable

Authentic friendships are built on honesty and transparency. Be open to sharing your experiences, struggles, and victories with others. Create a space where they feel comfortable doing the same. This mutual openness fosters trust and deepens your connections. Be there for each other in times of need, offering encouragement and assistance. Hold each other accountable in your spiritual walks, gently correcting and guiding one another toward Christ-like behavior. Focus on mutual trust, respect, and support.

Reflect Christ's Love

Strive to embody the love and grace of Jesus in your interactions. Be patient, kind, and forgiving, allowing your friendships to be a testament to the transformative power of God's love.

By intentionally pursuing these steps, you'll cultivate friendships that not only enrich your life but also glorify God. Remember, building godly relationships is a journey that requires effort, prayer, and a heart attuned to the leading of the Holy Spirit.

Disciple Others as You Grow

You don't need to be an expert. If you're one step ahead of someone in faith, you can walk with them. Invite a younger man in the faith to lunch. Read a book or study a book of the Bible together. Just start.

Discipleship isn't about having all the answers. It's about walking in truth, love, and humility, together.

Why Many Men Miss Out on Brotherhood

Let's be honest: many men are relationally isolated.

It is easy to fall into patterns. We've been taught to keep things surface-level.

Somewhere along the way, culture taught men to compete rather than connect, to stay guarded instead of opening up, and to protect an image instead of being real. That mindset slowly kills the chance for real brotherhood and shuts the door on meaningful discipleship.

Many men hold back because they are afraid of being judged if they are fully known. Others carry shame from past sins and wonder if anyone would still accept them.

Some believe the lie that no one would really understand what they are going through. Add to that the busyness of life, packed schedules, and the feeling of not even knowing how to start a deeper friendship, and isolation can easily become the default.

But isolation is a dangerous place. When you stay isolated, it becomes easier for sin to take root quietly. Shame festers when it stays hidden. Spiritual strength begins to weaken when you try to carry the weight of life alone.

God did not design you to walk your faith journey by yourself. Brotherhood is not just a good idea. It is a vital part of how God strengthens you, protects you, and grows you into the man He created you to be. Choosing to pursue real brotherhood is choosing the path of life, strength, and lasting growth.

In short, work towards resolving these reasons men stay isolated:

- Fear of being judged
- Shame over past sin
- Belief that "no one would understand"
- Busyness and lack of margin
- Not knowing how to start

Isolation is dangerous. It's where sin grows, shame festers, and spiritual strength weakens.

The Fruit of Brotherhood and Discipleship

When men walk together in truth and love, transformation happens. You begin to see:

- Real spiritual growth
- Lasting freedom from sin
- Greater clarity in your calling
- Confidence in your faith
- Joy in walking with Jesus and not alone, but alongside brothers who have your back

You also multiply your impact because discipleship reproduces.

As you grow and help others grow, they, in turn, do the same, and the ripple effect is powerful.

Ecclesiastes 4:12 (NIV): *"Though one may be overpowered, two can defend themselves. A cord of three strands is not quickly broken."*

How to Disciple Others Even If You Feel Unqualified

Stepping into the role of discipling others can feel daunting, especially when you question your own qualifications. It's common to think you lack the necessary knowledge or experience.

However, remember that Jesus chose ordinary individuals like fishermen, tax collectors, and everyday people to be His disciples and to carry His message forward.

Their effectiveness didn't stem from formal education or societal status but from their willingness to follow Him and share their experiences.

The essence of discipleship lies in genuine relationships and a shared journey toward Christ. It's not about having all the answers but about walking alongside others, learning together, and encouraging one another in faith. It is more about sharing than teaching, and in the sharing, you learn together.

Your personal experiences, both struggles and victories, can serve as powerful testimonies to those you mentor. By being authentic and transparent, you create an environment where others feel safe to open up and grow.

God often calls those who feel unprepared, equipping them along the way.

As you step out in faith, you'll find your perceived weaknesses become avenues for God's strength to manifest. Trust in His guidance, rely on His wisdom, and remember that your commitment and obedience are what truly matter.

By embracing this mindset, you allow God to work through you, impacting lives and advancing His kingdom.

Don't Walk Alone

The enemy loves isolated men. Isolation weakens. The enemy knows that a man standing alone is easier to deceive, easier to discourage, and easier to distract from his purpose. That is why he works so hard to keep men isolated. Brotherhood strengthens when men walk together, confessing sin, pursuing Jesus, and standing shoulder to shoulder. They become a force the darkness cannot easily withstand.

If you have been trying to walk alone, now is the time to make a different choice. You were never created to carry your burdens by yourself. You were made for connection. You were made for brotherhood. You were made to both receive strength from others and to give it.

Take the first step. Start the conversation you have been putting off. Reach out to someone. Pursue the connection you have been waiting for someone else to initiate. Be the man who steps up and invites another into the journey. Do not wait for perfect circumstances. Do not wait until you feel ready. Start where you are, and trust that God will honor your obedience.

Step into the mission of discipleship. Look for younger men who need encouragement. Walk closely with brothers who are heading toward Christ. Open your life so others can see how you are following Jesus, not perfectly, but faithfully. Every step you take toward brotherhood is a step toward strength, healing, and lasting impact.

Godly men do not just grow strong for themselves; they invest in others. They lift others up. They help others walk free. They multiply what God has done in them. You are called to be that kind of man. A man who refuses isolation. A man who builds brotherhood. A man who strengthens others as he continues to be strengthened by God. You were never meant to walk alone. Step into the life you were made for.

Chapter 13
Living a Missional Life

You Are on Assignment

Every man of God has a mission and it's not optional.

When Jesus saves a man, He doesn't just clean him up so he can sit in a pew and behave. He equips him to represent Christ and advance the Kingdom wherever he goes. You are not just saved *from* something you are saved *for* something.

The word *missional* simply means living with the awareness that your life is part of God's mission. It's about living intentionally, not accidentally. It means you understand that you are an ambassador, a messenger, and a servant of the King in every environment you're in, home, work, community, church, or even the gym.

2 Corinthians 5:20 (NIV) says, *"We are therefore Christ's ambassadors, as though God were making His appeal through us."* God is working through you. His strategy for reaching the world is pastors or missionaries and every believer living on mission.

This chapter is about helping you embrace your role as a man on assignment. We'll talk about:

- What it means to live missionally in everyday life
- How to share the gospel naturally and boldly
- Why your job, routine, and relationships are not random
- The connection between purpose and mission
- How to live as light in a dark world

You don't need to change careers or move overseas to live missionally. You need to open your eyes to the mission field that's already around you.

Discipleship vs Missional

As you've just learned about discipleship and are now preparing to learn about missional work, here is a comparison of the two which will help you avoid confusion.

Discipleship and being missional are two integral aspects of the Christian journey, each with its distinct focus yet deeply interconnected.

Discipleship involves the intentional process of learning from Jesus, embracing His teachings, and striving to reflect His character in every facet of life. It's about deepening one's relationship with Christ, growing in faith, and being transformed into His likeness. This journey often involves studying Scripture, engaging in prayer, and participating in a community of believers who encourage and challenge one another toward spiritual growth and maturity. And with it comes brotherhood.

Being missional, on the other hand, refers to actively living out and sharing one's faith in the world. It encompasses embodying the love and message of Christ in everyday interactions, seeking to serve others, and making disciples. Being missional means participating in God's redemptive work by reaching out to those who don't know Him, addressing societal needs, and reflecting God's kingdom through acts of compassion and justice.

While discipleship focuses on personal spiritual growth and formation, being missional emphasizes outward expression and engagement with the world. However, these two are not mutually exclusive; rather, they complement and fuel each other. As one grows in discipleship, understanding, and embodying Christ's teachings, there arises a natural inclination to be missional and to share the transformative power of the gospel with others. Conversely, engaging missionally can deepen one's discipleship, as it challenges and strengthens faith through real-world application.

In essence, a balanced Christian life involves both being a disciple and living missionally. This dual commitment ensures that faith is both nurtured internally and expressed externally, aligning with Jesus' call to love God wholeheartedly and love one's neighbor actively.

What Does It Mean to Live Missionally?

Living missionally means seeing every aspect of your life through the lens of God's purpose; in other words, living with spiritual awareness and eternal purpose. It is choosing to see every place you step into, every conversation you have, and every relationship you build as an opportunity to reflect the heart of Jesus and reveal His love to others.

Jesus described it simply and powerfully in Matthew 5:14-16 (NIV) when He said, *"You are the light of the world… let your light shine before others, that they may see your good deeds and glorify your Father in heaven."*

Living missionally is stepping into that calling to be a light. It is not about forcing conversations or preaching sermons at every opportunity. It is about living your faith openly, with courage and consistency, in a way that naturally points people toward God.

When you live missionally, your faith is not something you hide or compartmentalize. It is visible in how you work, how you serve, how you listen, how you respond under pressure, and how you love those around you. It becomes the lens through which you see your neighborhood, your workplace, your family, and your community.

Living missionally means living every day ready to be used by God, expecting that He is already working and inviting you to join Him in what He is doing. It means carrying the hope and truth of Jesus wherever you go.

You Are Where You Are on Purpose

You are not where you are by accident. Living missionally begins right where you are. Your family, job, gym, school, friends, colleagues, and neighbors are all part of your immediate mission field. By intentionally engaging with those around you, you can reflect Christ's love and make a meaningful impact.

Acts 17:26-27 (NIV) says, *"[God] marked out their appointed times in history and the boundaries of their lands. God did this so that they would seek Him..."*

Where you live and who you're around is part of a bigger plan. The question is: Are you paying attention to the opportunities around you?

Build Genuine Relationships

Take the time to know the people in your community. Show genuine interest in their lives, listen to their stories, and share your own. Authentic connections open doors for deeper conversations about faith and life.

Serve Others Selflessly

Look for opportunities to serve those around you. Whether it's helping a neighbor with errands, volunteering at local events, or simply offering a helping hand, acts of service demonstrate Christ's love in action.

Live Out Your Faith Consistently

Let your actions align with your beliefs. Exhibit integrity, kindness, and compassion in all areas of life. When others see the consistency between your faith and actions, it can inspire them to explore their own spiritual journey.

By embracing these practices, you become a living testament to God's grace and truth, profoundly impacting your immediate surroundings.

God wants to use your life, your story, and your transformation to spark curiosity and point people to Jesus.

How to Share the Gospel Boldly and Naturally

You do not need to be a preacher or a polished speaker to share your faith. What matters most is being real, intentional, and willing to seize opportunities as they come.

The first way to share your faith is to live differently. Before you ever say a word, let your life speak. Be the man who shows honesty, kindness, calm under pressure, and a heart that forgives quickly. People notice character that stands out in a world full of anger, selfishness, and pride. Living with integrity opens more doors than you might realize.

Building relationships is another key. Missional living always starts with presence. Be the man who knows people's names, asks real questions, and listens without rushing to give advice. Influence grows where trust and care have already been established. People are far more open to hearing about your faith when they know you genuinely care about them.

When the time comes, share your story. People may argue with theology or doctrine, but no one can argue with what God has done in your life.

Practice telling your story simply and honestly, in just a few minutes. You might say something like, "I used to be full of fear and anger, but when I surrendered my life to Jesus, He began to change me from the inside out."

Keep it real. Keep it personal. Keep it centered on what God has done, not on what you have achieved.

One powerful way to open a door for deeper conversation is by offering to pray. When someone shares a struggle or challenge they are facing, take a step of faith and ask, "Would it be okay if I prayed for you?"

You will be surprised at how many people say yes. Prayer often softens hearts and leads to more meaningful conversations about faith and hope.

Eventually, someone will ask you why you believe the way you do or what makes you different. Be ready to share the simple message of the gospel.

Tell them that God created us for a relationship with Him, that sin broke that relationship, and that Jesus came to restore it through His death and resurrection.

Remind them that salvation is a gift received by grace through faith, not something we earn, and encourage them that anyone who calls on Jesus will be saved, just as Romans 10:9-10 promises.

You do not need perfect words. You just need a heart that is willing to be bold and a love for people that drives you to share the hope you have found.

Your Work Is Your Mission Field

Faith is not something you leave behind when you walk into the office or the job site.

Too many men compartmentalize their faith and their work, but the truth is your workplace is one of your greatest mission fields. Your job is more than a paycheck. It is a platform.

Whatever your profession, whether you own a business, work a trade, sit in an office, or lead a team, you are a representative of God's Kingdom there. The way you work, the attitude you bring, the way you treat others, and the way you handle pressure all reveal who you belong to.

Colossians 3:23 (NIV) reminds us, *"Whatever you do, work at it with all your heart, as working for the Lord, not for human masters."* When you work with excellence, resolve conflict with grace, lead with integrity, and serve others with humility, people notice.

You do not need to wait for a better job or a more "spiritual" opportunity to live missionally. Your mission starts right where you are, with the people already around you.

God has placed you there on purpose. Shine your light in the place He has planted you.

Being Salt and Light in a Dark World

As we've explored the essence of living missionally, it's vital to understand the profound metaphors Jesus used to describe our role in the world: being the salt of the earth and the light of the world. These images encapsulate the impact we're called to have in our daily lives.

Being the Salt of the Earth

In the ancient world, salt served multiple purposes: it preserved food, enhanced flavor, and purified offerings. Similarly, as followers of Christ, we're called to preserve goodness, add value, and exemplify purity in our surroundings. By upholding integrity, promoting peace, and living out Christ's teachings, we act as a preserving agent against moral decay and a source of flavor that enriches the lives of those around us.

Being the Light of the World

Light dispels darkness and provides guidance. Jesus' declaration positions us as beacons in a world that is often overshadowed by confusion and despair. Our actions, words, and attitudes should illuminate the path to truth and hope. By reflecting God's love and righteousness, we offer direction and clarity to others, encouraging them to seek and glorify God.

Embracing our roles as salt and light means actively engaging with the world in a transformative way. It's about living authentically, demonstrating Christ's love through deeds, and being unwavering in our commitment to His principles. Through such a life, we not only fulfill our divine calling but also inspire others to recognize and honor God.

Missional Living Produces Eternal Impact

You can't live on mission if your life is overloaded with busyness. You need space for divine interruptions. Space to notice people. Space to slow down and care.

Jesus lived missionally *with margin*. He noticed the woman at the well. He stopped for blind men. He paused to heal, bless, and listen.

Living on mission is about being aware of *why you're here* and *who's around you*.

At the end of your life, your resume won't matter. Your bank account won't matter. The size of your house won't matter.

What will matter is how you lived for the mission of Jesus.

Did you love people well? Did you share the hope of the gospel? Did you use your influence to serve, not just succeed?

When you live missionally:

- People get introduced to Jesus
- Eternities are changed
- Your own faith comes alive
- Your life becomes part of something much bigger than yourself

One day, you'll hear:

"Well done, good and faithful servant." (Matthew 25:23)

You're a Missionary–Right Where You Are

You don't need to fly across the world to live on mission. You just need to open your eyes, listen to the Spirit, and take action in faith.

Start with a neighbor. A coworker. A friend. A stranger God nudges you to talk to.

Ask God daily:

"Who do You want me to notice today? Who needs hope? Who needs Jesus?"

Then trust that He'll lead you. And walk in the power He's already given you.

Because the world doesn't just need more religious men—it needs men **on mission**, filled with the Spirit, willing to step into darkness with the light of Christ.

That's you.

Remember, embracing a missional life means integrating your faith into every aspect of your daily routine. It's about recognizing that your workplace, neighborhood, and social circles are all arenas where you can reflect Christ's love and grace. By living authentically and intentionally, you become a beacon of hope and a testament to the transformative power of the Gospel.

As you continue this journey, remember that living missionally doesn't require grand gestures or far-off missions. It starts with simple, everyday actions: showing kindness to a coworker, lending a listening ear to a friend, or extending grace in challenging situations. These moments, though seemingly small, collectively create a profound impact.

Reflect on the opportunities before you. How can you embody the love of Christ in your current environment? Who in your life needs to experience His grace through your actions? By answering these questions and stepping out in faith, you align yourself with God's mission and open the door to transformative experiences for both yourself and those around you.

Living a missional life is an ongoing journey of faith, courage, and intentionality. As you walk this path, trust that God will equip and guide you, using your unique gifts and experiences to further His kingdom. Embrace the call, step into the mission field that is your everyday life, and witness the incredible ways God can work through you.

Part V
Perseverance and Legacy

Introduction: Finishing Strong Matters

Spiritual growth is profoundly measured by the steadfastness of your journey and the strength with which you conclude. Many embark on their walk with God filled with zeal and dedication.

However, as life's challenges arise, things like trials, mounting pressures, and fatigue, there's a risk of waning passion or drifting from one's divine purpose.

Without cultivating spiritual perseverance, it's easy to settle for a diluted version of the abundant life God envisions for you.

The Christian path was never promised to be devoid of hardships.

Yet, God assures His unwavering presence through every storm, offering the strength to remain resolute, faithful, and to craft a legacy that glorifies Him.

As James 1:12 (NIV) reminds us:

"Blessed is the one who perseveres under trial because, having stood the test, that person will receive the crown of life that the Lord has promised to those who love him."

This concluding section delves into the essence of enduring faith. It emphasizes:

- Strategies to remain unwavering during life's trials
- The significance of completing your spiritual journey with vigor
- Ways to establish a legacy that resonates beyond your lifetime

The Christian life mirrors a marathon more than a sprint. It is a continuous pursuit of Christ. It's not about flawless execution but about persistent faithfulness. The man who endures, navigating challenges with grace and determination, leaves an indelible mark on the world and in the hearts of those he touches.

Let's embark on understanding where this endurance is most profoundly shaped: amidst life's trials.

Chapter 14
Standing Firm in Trials

Trials Are Not the End of the Story

If you are not facing a trial right now, chances are you have just come out of one, or one is on the way. Life in a broken world guarantees it. Every man, no matter how strong his faith, will encounter pressure, pain, and difficulty. Following Jesus does not exempt you from suffering. In fact, walking with Christ often brings even more resistance because you are choosing a narrow path in a world that prefers the wide one.

The good news is this: you are never alone in the fire. Your pain is never wasted. God does not abandon you in trials. He meets you in them. He strengthens you through them. And He refines your character so that you come out stronger, purer, and more anchored in Him.

Peter reminds us in 1 Peter 4:12-13 (NIV): *"Dear friends, do not be surprised at the fiery ordeal that has come on you to test you... But rejoice inasmuch as you participate in the sufferings of Christ..."* Trials are not punishments. They are proving grounds. They are the places where your faith is tested, your heart is purified, and your spiritual endurance is built. When you stand firm in the middle of the struggle, you grow roots that reach deeper into God's truth, and you bear fruit that will last.

This chapter is about helping you face trials with courage instead of fear. We will look at the purpose behind your struggles and how God uses them for your growth. You will learn how to stay grounded when life feels shaky and how to grab hold of the promises of God that will keep you steady. You will discover habits and mindsets that help you remain faithful even when everything around you tries to pull you off course.

Most importantly, you will learn how to shift your mindset. Instead of asking, "Why me?" you will start asking, "God, how can you use this?" Because trials are not the end of your story. They are the training ground for the strength you will need to fulfill the calling God has placed on your life.

In short, this chapter will help you:

- Understand the purpose of trials in your spiritual growth
- Learn how to stay grounded when life is shaking
- Discover the promises of God that hold you steady
- Develop habits and perspectives that keep you faithful
- Shift your mindset from "why me?" to "use this"

The trials you face are not the end of your story. They are forging the man you are becoming and when you learn to stand firm, you do not just survive the hard seasons. They're the place where your strength is forged and your faith becomes unshakable.

Faith Refined: Embracing Trials as Pathways to Spiritual Maturity

God Uses Trials to Refine, Not Destroy.

The Christian journey is fraught with trials. While they often bring discomfort and uncertainty, they serve a divine purpose in our spiritual development.

What is that purpose, you say? Well, God is omniscient, so He does not need to "try" us to see what we will do ... he already knows. Therefore, the trials must be for us. We can then know of what we are capable, and are then able to share with others so they too can understand.

The Scriptures illuminate this transformative process, encouraging believers to perceive challenges not as mere obstacles but as opportunities for growth and deepened faith.

James 1:2-4 (NIV) offers profound insight:

"Consider it pure joy, my brothers and sisters, whenever you face trials of many kinds, because you know that the testing of your faith produces perseverance. Let perseverance finish its work so that you may be mature and complete, not lacking anything."

This passage underscores a counterintuitive yet transformative perspective: embracing trials with joy.

Such an approach recognizes that these challenges are instrumental in cultivating perseverance, a steadfastness that fortifies our character and propels us toward spiritual maturity.

Similarly, Romans 5:3-5 (NIV) reinforces this notion:

"Not only so, but we also glory in our sufferings, because we know that suffering produces perseverance; perseverance, character; and character, hope."

Here, the Apostle Paul talks about where suffering leads to hope. The endurance experienced through trials refines our character, and this refined character becomes a hope that does not disappoint.

It's essential to recognize that God does not orchestrate all suffering, but He permits it, ensuring that no pain is without purpose.

Trials act to purify our faith, much like gold is refined by fire. This refining process strips away impurities, revealing a faith that is genuine and resilient.

Enduring hardships with faith yields multifaceted benefits:

- **Deepened Trust in God**: Navigating life's storms compels us to rely more profoundly on God's wisdom and strength, fostering an intimate relationship with Him.

- **Strengthened Character**: Consistently facing and overcoming challenges molds our moral and spiritual fiber, aligning us more closely with Christ's image.

- **Enhanced Empathy**: Personal experiences of suffering sensitize us to the plights of others, equipping us to offer genuine compassion and support.

- **Unwavering Hope**: Recognizing God's faithfulness in past trials fortifies our confidence in His promises, anchoring us in hope for the future.

In embracing trials as divine instruments of refinement, we participate in a transformative journey. This journey not only shapes us into the individuals God intends us to be but also prepares us to fulfill our purpose with authenticity and grace.

How to Stand Firm When the Pressure Hits

When life presses in and everything feels unstable, standing firm begins with staying anchored in God's Word. In the middle of a storm, opinions and emotions can toss you around. You need something stronger to hold onto. Scripture becomes that anchor. Psalm 119:92 (NIV) reminds us, *"If your law had not been my delight, I would have perished in my affliction."* God's Word steadies your heart when your circumstances scream confusion. His promises give you something unshakable to stand on, especially when life does not make sense.

Prayer is another place where strength is built. You may not always feel like praying during a trial, but that is exactly when prayer is most powerful.

Keep showing up. Talk to God honestly, even if all you can bring Him is your fear, your frustration, or your fatigue. Romans 12:12 (NIV) encourages us, *"Be joyful in hope, patient in affliction, faithful in prayer."*

God is not looking for perfect words. He is looking for your presence, your honesty, and your willingness to lean on Him.

You also need people around you who will help you carry the load. Trials are not the time to isolate yourself. They are the time to lean into brotherhood. Let godly men stand with you, pray for you, and speak truth when your own vision is blurred by pain.

Galatians 6:2 (NIV) says, *"Carry each other's burdens, and in this way you will fulfill the law of Christ."* Brotherhood strengthens you when your own strength feels low.

In the middle of pressure, it is easy to forget what is true. That is why you must remind yourself daily of who you are and whose you are. God is still good. God is still with you. You are still His son.

The storm you are facing will not last forever. When you hold onto your identity in Christ, you anchor your soul to something that does not move.

Finally, while it is right and good to ask God to bring relief, it is just as important to ask Him to use the trial to shape you.

Jesus Himself asked the Father to remove the cup of suffering if possible, but He also submitted to God's greater purpose.

You can pray the same way. Ask, "God, what do You want to do in me through this?" When your focus shifts from escaping the trial to growing through it, the hardship becomes holy ground. It becomes the place where God does some of His deepest, most lasting work in your life.

Trials are not just something to survive. They are places where endurance is forged, character is formed, and your faith becomes unshakable.

1. Stay Anchored in God's Word

In a storm, you need an anchor. Scripture holds you steady when your emotions and circumstances try to shake you.

Psalm 119:92 (NIV): *"If your law had not been my delight, I would have perished in my affliction."*

Make God's Word your foundation, especially when things don't make sense.

2. Keep Showing Up in Prayer

You may not always feel inspired to pray in a trial. That's okay. Pray anyway. Talk to God honestly. Let Him meet you in your frustration, fear, and fatigue.

Romans 12:12 (NIV): *"Be joyful in hope, patient in affliction, faithful in prayer."*

God wants your presence and your honesty.

3. Surround Yourself with Godly Brothers

Trials are when you need brotherhood most. Don't isolate. Invite others in. Let them carry the load with you, pray for you, and remind you of truth when your vision is blurred.

Galatians 6:2 (NIV): *"Carry each other's burdens, and in this way you will fulfill the law of Christ."*

4. Remember Who You Are and Whose You Are

When everything feels uncertain, go back to what you know:

- God is still good (Psalm 34:8)
- God is still with you (Isaiah 43:2)
- You are still His son (Romans 8:16-17)
- This storm will not last forever (2 Corinthians 4:17)

Identity anchors you in chaos.

5. Ask God to Use It, Not Just Remove It

It's okay to ask for relief. Jesus did (Matthew 26:39). But also ask, *"God, what do You want to do in me through this?"*

When your perspective shifts from **escape** to **transformation**, the trial becomes holy ground.

What Standing Firm Looks Like

Standing firm doesn't mean pretending everything is okay. It doesn't mean you never cry, question, or wrestle.

It means:

- You don't quit.
- You keep trusting, even when you don't understand.
- You refuse to let the enemy steal your joy or derail your faith.
- You hold your position planted in the truth, eyes on Jesus.

Ephesians 6:13 (NIV): *"Therefore put on the full armor of God… so that when the day of evil comes, you may be able to stand your ground, and after you have done everything, to stand."*

Sometimes standing is the victory. Trusting God through storms.

Your Trial Is Part of Your Testimony

The pain you're walking through now may one day be the very story that sets someone else free. Your endurance may become the encouragement another man needs. Your scars can become a source of strength for others.

2 Corinthians 1:3-4 (NIV): *"[God] comforts us in all our troubles, so that we can comfort those in any trouble with the comfort we ourselves receive from God."*

Nothing is wasted. Every trial, every tear, every unanswered question can be used by God to shape your character and amplify your impact.

Hold the Line

Whatever you're going through, hold the line.

God is not finished. His promises still stand. And your trial is not the end of your story.

- Stay in the Word.
- Stay in prayer.
- Stay connected to your brothers.
- Stay rooted in your identity.
- Stay faithful, one day at a time.

You're going to survive this and you're going to be stronger because of it, because godly men grow in the light, and they grow deep in the dark.

Promises of God

When navigating the turbulent waters of life's trials, it's essential to anchor ourselves in the unwavering promises of God. These divine assurances provide not only solace but also strength, guiding us through challenges with renewed hope and confidence.

God's Presence in Our Struggles

One of the most profound promises is that God remains with us during our hardships. In Isaiah 41:10 (NIV), He declares:

"So do not fear, for I am with you; do not be dismayed, for I am your God. I will strengthen you and help you; I will uphold you with my righteous right hand."

This assurance reminds us that we're never alone; God's steadfast presence offers both comfort and strength.

Purpose Behind the Pain

Trials, while challenging, serve a greater purpose in our spiritual growth. Romans 5:3-5 (NIV) elucidates this process:

"Not only so, but we also glory in our sufferings, because we know that suffering produces perseverance; perseverance, character; and character, hope."

These verses highlight the transformative power of hardships, molding our character and deepening our hope.

Divine Deliverance and Restoration

God's commitment to our well-being includes deliverance from afflictions. Psalm 34:19 (NIV) assures us:

"The righteous person may have many troubles, but the Lord delivers him from them all."

Furthermore, Psalm 71:20 (NIV) speaks to restoration:

"Though you have made me see troubles, many and bitter, you will restore my life again; from the depths of the earth you will again bring me up."

These promises affirm that our trials are temporary and God's deliverance is certain.

Enduring Love and Unfailing Support

In moments of weakness, God's love becomes our stronghold.

Romans 8:38-39 (NIV) emphasizes the inseparability of His love:

"For I am convinced that neither death nor life, neither angels nor demons, neither the present nor the future, nor any powers... will be able to separate us from the love of God that is in Christ Jesus our Lord."

This profound truth offers unwavering assurance amidst life's uncertainties.

By internalizing and meditating on these promises, we equip ourselves to face trials not with fear, but with faith. God's Word serves as a beacon, illuminating our path and reminding us of His eternal commitment to our journey.

In the journey of faith, trials are not obstacles but opportunities for growth and deeper reliance on God. By anchoring ourselves in His Word, maintaining a steadfast prayer life, and surrounding ourselves with a supportive community, we can navigate life's challenges with resilience and grace.

Remember, as 1 Corinthians 16:13 (NIV) encourages:

"Be on your guard; stand firm in the faith; be courageous; be strong."

Embracing this mindset transforms trials into refining moments, shaping us into the individuals God intends us to be.

Chapter 15
Finishing the Race Well

The Significance of Your Finish

Life is often likened to a race, and each of us is a runner on this course. While many may begin with enthusiasm and determination, it's the endurance and faithfulness displayed throughout the journey that truly define our legacy. Some may sprint ahead only to lose momentum, and others might veer off track, but a select few remain steadfast, pressing forward with unwavering focus until the very end.

God doesn't seek perfection in us; He desires faithfulness. He values those who, despite obstacles and hardships, refuse to give up, continually rise after each fall, and stay the course even when the path is arduous or lonely.

The Apostle Paul, reflecting on his own journey, encapsulates this sentiment in 2 Timothy 4:7-8 (NIV):

"I have fought the good fight, I have finished the race, I have kept the faith. Now there is in store for me the crown of righteousness..."

This chapter discusses the essence of finishing strong and living a life marked by faithfulness. It's about maintaining an eternal perspective, making the most of the time we've been given, and leaving behind a legacy characterized by integrity, conviction, and courage.

Remember, the impact of your life isn't solely determined by how you start, but more importantly, by how you finish. The choices you make in your later years, the consistency of your character, and the quiet moments of perseverance often speak louder than the initial enthusiasm of your youth.

In this chapter, we will explore:

- The true meaning of finishing well in the eyes of God
- Common pitfalls that can hinder a strong finish
- Strategies to stay motivated when the journey becomes challenging
- Prioritizing what holds eternal significance
- Living each day, keeping the finish in mind

While beginning the race requires initiative and energy, it's the faithful and steadfast completion that leaves a lasting impact.

What Does It Mean to Finish Well?

Finishing centers on embodying key virtues that reflect a life devoted to God's calling:

- **Faithfulness**: Consistently showing up and remaining obedient to God's directives, regardless of the circumstances. It's about steadfast commitment to His will throughout life's seasons.
- **Endurance**: Persevering through hardships without yielding. This involves maintaining trust in God's plan, even when faced with trials that test one's resolve.
- **Integrity**: Upholding moral and ethical principles, choosing righteousness over convenience, and ensuring that one's actions align with God's standards.

- **Legacy**: Imparting truth, love, wisdom, and a godly example to others. It's about influencing lives in a manner that honors God and perpetuates His teachings.

At life's conclusion, the measure is in the faithfulness with which one has stewarded God's gifts and callings. This sentiment is echoed in Matthew 25:21 (NIV), where the master commends his servant:

"Well done, good and faithful servant! You have been faithful with a few things; I will put you in charge of many things."

This verse shows that God values our faithfulness in the responsibilities He entrusts to us, no matter their scale. The ultimate goal is to live in such a way that we hear these affirming words from our Lord, signifying a race well run and a life well lived in His service.

Threats That Can Derail Your Finish

Men rarely fall because of one big decision. They fall because of slow compromise over time. Stay alert to these common threats:

1. Spiritual Apathy

As life settles into routine, some men start coasting. The fire dies out. They stop pursuing God with hunger. They stop growing. Comfort becomes king.

Stay hungry. Keep pursuing God like you did at the beginning. Don't coast into spiritual retirement.

2. Isolation

Older men often withdraw. They believe the lie that they've already "done their part" and now it's someone else's turn. But your wisdom and presence are needed more than ever.

Stay connected. Keep pouring into others. Keep receiving from others. Keep showing up.

3. Bitterness or Disappointment

Over time, wounds can harden your heart. Failed dreams, broken relationships, or unanswered prayers can make a man cynical or cold.

Stay soft. Keep forgiving. Keep trusting God's goodness, even when life doesn't unfold the way you expected.

4. Moral Failure

Some men let their guard down late in life. They get tired, bored, or entitled and make devastating decisions that cost them their legacy.

Stay alert. Finish your race with integrity. Guard your heart to the end.

How to Stay Strong to the End

1. Keep Your Eyes on Jesus

Hebrews 12:1-2 (NIV): *"Let us run with perseverance the race marked out for us, fixing our eyes on Jesus, the pioneer and perfecter of faith…"*

Your focus determines your endurance. Don't focus on how far you have left. Focus on Jesus–His faithfulness, His grace, and His power to carry you.

2. Stay in the Word and Prayer

You never outgrow the basics. The Word keeps you grounded. Prayer keeps you connected. These habits are your fuel–don't let them slip.

3. Invest in the Next Generation

You finish well by passing the baton. Pour into younger men. Tell your story. Share your failures and your wisdom. Help someone else run their race better.

Psalm 71:18 (NIV): *"Even when I am old and gray, do not forsake me, my God, till I declare your power to the next generation…"*

4. Keep Saying Yes to God

Your calling doesn't end until you see Him face-to-face. Keep saying yes to whatever God puts in front of you—whether it's serving, mentoring, praying, giving, or encouraging.

What Kind of Legacy Will You Leave?

Your legacy isn't what you leave **for** people—it's what you leave **in** people.

Your children, your wife, your friends, your coworkers—what will they remember about how you lived, loved, served, and finished?

You don't have to be wealthy, famous, or impressive. You just have to be faithful.

Live so that when your time is up, the people who knew you say:

- "He loved Jesus."
- "He led with courage and humility."
- "He never quit."
- "He made me better."
- "He finished strong."

That's a legacy worth building.

Run to the Finish Line

You may be tired. You may have scars. You may have failed along the way. But you're still in the race.

So run.

Run with your eyes on Jesus.
Run with purpose.
Run with endurance.
Run for the ones behind you.
Run knowing the crown of righteousness is waiting.

Because when the final chapter of your story is written, you don't want it to end with *almost*.
You want it to end with faith.

Conclusion
Empowered for a Life that Honors God

You weren't just called to survive this life—you were called to live it with strength, clarity, and impact, all for the glory of God.

This entire journey through identity, discipline, holiness, leadership, and perseverance has been about one thing: helping you live the kind of life that honors God.

You won't just honor God with your words, but with your choices, priorities, relationships, habits, and influence.

And the truth is, you already have what you need.

You have the Word of God.
You have the Spirit of God.
You have the people of God.
You have the authority of Christ.
You have the call of God on your life.

You are not powerless. You are not disqualified. You are not forgotten.
You are a man of God, and you are empowered to live like it.

This doesn't mean life will be easy. It means you've been given everything you need for godliness and spiritual victory (2 Peter 1:3).

You can walk in freedom. You can lead your family. You can resist temptation. You can pray with power. You can disciple others. You can finish well.

Not because you're perfect but because you're empowered by the One who is.

Living a life that honors God isn't about pretending to be strong. It's about being dependent on Him, daily. It's about waking up and saying, *"Lord, lead me today. Use me. Shape me. Strengthen me. I belong to You."*

When you live that way, humbly, courageously, and intentionally, you bring glory to God, and you become a man the world desperately needs: grounded, unshakable, and full of fire.

So don't shrink back. Don't coast. Don't settle for less.

Step into the life you were made for. Not just a life of belief, but a life of power. A life that reflects the greatness of the God you serve.

A Final Charge to Men of Faith

Brother, you've been called to something greater.

More than a church attendee and more than someone who manages your sin or maintains your image, but to be a faithful man of God, equipped for spiritual battle, rooted in truth, marked by obedience, and filled with power.

The world doesn't need more passive men. It needs men who pray, men who lead, men who finish what they started. It needs men who are unashamed of the gospel and unshaken by the culture.

You are that man.

You've learned who you are in Christ. You've been equipped with the tools of spiritual discipline. You've faced the reality of warfare. You've embraced the call to lead and to live with mission. You've been reminded of the legacy you're building and the God who is building you.

Now, here's the charge:

Stand firm. Don't back down when it gets hard. Don't compromise when it would be easier. Don't quit when the process is slow. Keep your eyes on Jesus. Keep your heart humble. Keep your hands open to whatever He asks of you.

Lead well. Love your wife. Raise your kids with truth and grace. Lead in your home, your work, your community, and your church. Be the example that points people to Jesus, not through perfection, but through consistency.

Fight hard. Don't coast spiritually. Keep your armor on. Keep your sword sharp. Stay in the Word, stay in prayer, stay in brotherhood. When the enemy attacks, respond with faith, not fear.

Finish strong. Don't just live saved—live sent. Don't just start the race—finish it. Leave a legacy that honors Christ and makes it easier for the next generation to follow Him.

Finally...

Remember who you are:

You are a son of the King.
You are forgiven, chosen, called, and equipped.
You are filled with the Spirit of God.
You are not alone.
You are not weak.
You are not without purpose.

You are a man of faith, and the time to live like it is now.

Go. Lead. Fight. Love. Serve. Grow. Finish.

And may your life bring honor to the One who gave it all for you.

Afterword

As we conclude this journey through *Warrior: A Man's Guide to Spiritual Power and Purpose*, I want to express my deepest gratitude for walking this path with me. This book was born out of a desire to see men rise up—not in their own strength, but in the strength that comes from a life surrendered to God.

Throughout these pages, we've explored the foundations of spiritual growth, the disciplines that fortify our faith, the battles we must face for holiness, the call to lead and impact with power, and the importance of perseverance and legacy.

Each section was carefully crafted to equip you with the tools and insights necessary to navigate life's complexities with unwavering faith and purpose. Beyond the strategies and teachings, my hope is that you've encountered a renewed sense of identity—that you've recognized yourself as a warrior in God's kingdom, called to stand firm, to fight the good fight, and to lead others with integrity and love.

Remember, the journey doesn't end here. The true test of a warrior is not in the reading but in the doing. It's in the daily decisions to seek God, to serve others, and to stand firm in the face of adversity. It's in the legacy you build through consistent, faithful living.

As you move forward, may you continue to embrace your role as a spiritual warrior. May you find strength in God's Word, courage in His promises, and purpose in His calling. And when challenges arise—as they surely will—may you stand firm, knowing that you are equipped, empowered, and never alone.

Thank you for allowing me to be a part of your journey. Now, go forth and live the life of purpose and power that you were created for. With gratitude and encouragement.

Appendices

APPENDIX: 90-Day Bible Reading Plan

30-Day Bible Reading Plan for Spiritual Growth and Power

Day	Theme	Scripture	Focus
1	Identity in Christ	2 Corinthians 5:17	New creation in Christ
2	Crucified with Christ	Galatians 2:20	Living from Christ's life
3	The Word's Authority	2 Timothy 3:16-17	Trusting God's Word
4	Living by God's Word	Psalm 119:9-11	Purity through Scripture
5	Power of the Cross	Colossians 2:13-15	Christ's victory over sin
6	Grace Over Guilt	Romans 8:1-4	Freedom from condemnation
7	Power in Prayer	James 5:16-18	Effectiveness in prayer
8	The Lord's Prayer	Matthew 6:5-13	How Jesus taught us to pray
9	Fasting with Purpose	Matthew 6:16-18	Seeking God through fasting
10	Hungering for God	Psalm 63:1-8	Deep desire for God's presence
11	Worship and Praise	Psalm 100	Entering His presence with praise
12	Worship as a Weapon	Acts 16:25-26	Praising in the battle
13	Obedience and Trust	John 14:15	Love through obedience
14	Trusting God's Way	Proverbs 3:5-6	Leaning on God, not self
15	Spiritual Armor	Ephesians 6:10-18	Equipped for the battle

16	Standing Strong	1 Peter 5:8-10	Resist and stand firm
17	Resisting Temptation	1 Corinthians 10:13	A way of escape
18	Walking by the Spirit	Galatians 5:16-25	Living with Spirit-led power
19	Breaking Strongholds	2 Corinthians 10:3-5	Taking thoughts captive
20	Renewing the Mind	Romans 12:1-2	Transformation through renewal
21	Leading with Humility	Luke 22:24-27	Leading by serving
22	Godly Leadership	1 Timothy 3:1-13	Character in leadership
23	Discipleship Model	Matthew 28:18-20	The Great Commission
24	Brotherhood and Unity	Ecclesiastes 4:9-12	Strength in community
25	Living on Mission	2 Corinthians 5:17-21	Ambassadors for Christ
26	Let Your Light Shine	Matthew 5:13-16	Influence with purpose
27	Joy in Trials	James 1:2-4	Growth through hardship
28	God's Comfort in Suffering	2 Corinthians 1:3-7	Comforted to comfort others
29	Running the Race	Hebrews 12:1-3	Endurance and focus
30	Finishing Faithfully	2 Timothy 4:6-8	The crown of righteousness
31	God's Strength in Weakness	2 Corinthians 12:7-10	His grace is sufficient
32	Guarding Your Heart	Proverbs 4:20-27	Staying on the right path
33	Confession and Freedom	James 5:16	Healing through honesty

34	Seeking God First	Matthew 6:31-34	Priorities and provision
35	Freedom in Christ	Galatians 5:1	Stand firm in liberty
36	Daily Dying to Self	Luke 9:23-26	Following Christ completely
37	Patience in Process	Romans 5:1-5	Perseverance produces hope
38	God's Discipline as Love	Hebrews 12:5-11	Growing through correction
39	Humility Before Honor	Philippians 2:3-11	The mindset of Christ
40	God as Father	Psalm 103:8-14	God's compassion and mercy
41	Loving Your Wife	Ephesians 5:25-33	Christlike love in marriage
42	Teaching the Next Generation	Deuteronomy 6:4-9	Discipleship at home
43	Living with Integrity	Psalm 15	The character of a godly man
44	Honesty and Truthfulness	Proverbs 12:17-22	The power of truthful lips
45	Being a Man of Peace	Romans 12:14-21	Responding with grace
46	Stewarding Your Gifts	1 Peter 4:10-11	Using what God has entrusted
47	Being Faithful in the Small	Luke 16:10	Trust starts with little things
48	A Life That Bears Fruit	John 15:1-8	Abiding and fruitfulness
49	Persevering in Prayer	Luke 18:1-8	Don't give up praying
50	Guarding Against Pride	1 Peter 5:5-7	God lifts the humble
51	God's Plan and Purpose	Jeremiah 29:11-13	Seeking with all your heart

#	Title	Reference	Theme
52	Faith That Acts	James 2:14-26	Faith shown through obedience
53	Wisdom for Daily Life	Proverbs 3:1-8	Trust and direction
54	Walking in the Light	1 John 1:5-10	Confession and cleansing
55	Bearing with Others	Colossians 3:12-17	Compassion and community
56	God's Faithfulness	Lamentations 3:21-26	Hope in God's mercy
57	Being Watchful	Matthew 26:36-41	Stay awake and pray
58	Living for Eternity	2 Corinthians 4:16-18	Fix your eyes on the unseen
59	The Power of Your Words	Proverbs 18:20-21	Speak life, not death
60	Legacy and Reward	Revelation 2:10	Be faithful to the end
61	Maturity Through the Word	Hebrews 5:11-14	Growing from milk to meat
62	Seeking Wisdom	James 1:5-8	Asking without doubting
63	A Pure Heart Before God	Psalm 51:1-12	The prayer of repentance
64	Living a Holy Life	1 Peter 1:13-16	Be holy as God is holy
65	Strength in Surrender	Romans 6:11-14	Dead to sin, alive in Christ
66	Walking with God Consistently	Micah 6:6-8	What the Lord requires
67	Living with Purpose	Ephesians 2:8-10	Saved for good works
68	The Fear of the Lord	Proverbs 1:7	Foundation for wisdom

69	God's Guidance and Counsel	Psalm 32:6-11	Instruction from the Lord
70	Repentance and Restoration	Acts 3:19-21	Times of refreshing
71	Servant Leadership	John 13:1-17	Leading by washing feet
72	The Example of Paul	1 Corinthians 11:1	Follow me as I follow Christ
73	Endurance and Reward	Revelation 3:10-12	Hold on to what you have
74	Strengthening Others	1 Thessalonians 5:11-15	Encourage one another
75	Living Quietly and Purposefully	1 Thessalonians 4:9-12	Work with your hands
76	Suffering with Christ	Romans 8:16-18	Future glory outweighs present pain
77	Freedom from Condemnation	John 8:1-11	Grace and truth to the fallen
78	Consistent Character	Titus 2:6-8	Sound doctrine and self-control
79	Humility in Correction	Proverbs 27:5-6, 17	Faithful wounds of a friend
80	Guarding Your Mind	Philippians 4:6-9	Peace through prayer and focus
81	Faith to Move Forward	Joshua 1:7-9	Be strong and courageous
82	God's Provision	Philippians 4:10-13, 19	Contentment and supply
83	Dealing with Temptation Honestly	Psalm 19:12-14	Cleanse me from hidden faults
84	Remaining in the Vine	John 15:9-17	Abide in His love

85	The Power of the Gospel	Romans 1:16-17	Not ashamed of the good news
86	Prayer and Intercession	1 Timothy 2:1-8	Lifting others in prayer
87	Staying the Course	Galatians 6:7-10	Don't grow weary in doing good
88	Strength in Community	Acts 2:42-47	Devoted to fellowship and growth
89	Living with Vision	Habakkuk 2:1-4	Waiting with expectation
90	Finishing Faithfully	Revelation 21:1-7	Eternal reward and final victory

APPENDIX: Accepting Christ

Accepting Christ: Beginning Your Journey of Faith

Every warrior's journey begins with a pivotal decision–a moment of surrender that leads to transformation. Accepting Jesus Christ as your Lord and Savior is that defining moment. It's not merely a ritual or a recitation; it's the commencement of a profound relationship with the One who offers true strength, purpose, and redemption.

In the pages ahead, you'll find a prayer designed to guide you in this life-changing commitment. If your heart is ready, let these words be the bridge between your past and the victorious path that lies ahead.

Following the prayer, we've outlined essential next steps to help you grow in your newfound faith. From immersing yourself in God's Word to connecting with a community of fellow believers, these actions will equip you to stand firm, lead with integrity, and live out your calling with courage.

Remember, this is not the end–it's the beginning of your greatest adventure. Welcome to the brotherhood.

Prayer to Accept Christ as Lord and Savior

Heavenly Father,

I come to You today knowing that I need You.
I admit that I have sinned, and I've tried to live life my own way.
I believe that Jesus Christ is Your Son, that He died for my sins, and that He rose again from the dead.
I believe that through Him, I can be forgiven, made new, and brought into a right relationship with You.

So right now, I turn away from my sin.
I surrender my heart, my life, and my future to You.
Jesus, I invite You to be my **Lord** and my **Savior**.
Come into my life. Fill me with Your Holy Spirit.
Change me from the inside out.
Lead me in Your truth and teach me to follow You all the days of my life.

Thank You for saving me.
Thank You for loving me.
Thank You for making me a child of God.

In Jesus' name,
Amen.

Next Steps After Accepting Christ

A Guide to Help You Grow in Your New Faith

---

1. Celebrate the Most Important Decision of Your Life

If you just gave your life to Jesus, **heaven is celebrating** and so are we (Luke 15:7)! You are now a **child of God** (John 1:12), completely forgiven, deeply loved, and made new.

"Therefore, if anyone is in Christ, the new creation has come: The old has gone, the new is here!" –2 Corinthians 5:17 (NIV)

---

2. Start Reading the Bible Daily

God's Word is your foundation for truth, direction, and growth. Start here:

Recommended Starting Point:

- **Gospel of John** - to understand who Jesus is and what He did for you
- Then read **Romans** - to learn what salvation means and how to live by grace
- Then go to **Ephesians**, **James**, and **1 Peter** for practical daily Christian living

Bible Plan:

Use the 30-day or 90-day reading plan from *Warrior: A Man's Guide to Spiritual Power and Purpose* or start with this short plan:

- Day 1: John 1

- Day 2: John 3
- Day 3: Romans 5
- Day 4: Romans 8
- Day 5: Ephesians 2

📖 **Tip**: Try reading one chapter a day. Before reading, pray:

"Lord, speak to me through Your Word. Help me understand and live what I read."

---

3. Talk to God Daily Through Prayer

Prayer is a conversation with your Heavenly Father. You don't need fancy words–just honesty and consistency.

Start with this simple model (ACTS):

- **A**doration - Praise God for who He is
- **C**onfession - Admit where you've fallen short
- **T**hanksgiving - Thank Him for His grace and blessings
- **S**upplication - Ask Him for what you need and pray for others

"Devote yourselves to prayer, being watchful and thankful."
–Colossians 4:2 (NIV)

---

4. Get Connected to a Bible-Based Church

God didn't design you to grow alone. Find a local church where:

- The Bible is taught clearly

- Jesus is honored as Lord
- Community and discipleship are encouraged
- There's a place for you to grow and serve

Ask a Christian friend or search online for a **Bible-teaching, Christ-centered church** in your area.

"Let us not give up meeting together… but encouraging one another…"–Hebrews 10:25 (NIV)

---

5. Get Baptized

Baptism is an outward expression of the inward change Christ has made in you. It doesn't save you, but it's your first step of obedience to publicly declare your new life in Christ.

Talk to your church or pastor about being baptized soon.

"Repent and be baptized… in the name of Jesus Christ for the forgiveness of your sins."–Acts 2:38 (NIV)

---

6. Build Godly Relationships

You need **brothers in Christ** to walk with you, challenge you, and encourage you.

- Join a men's group or Bible study at your church
- Find a mature believer to mentor you (discipleship)
- Be honest, teachable, and willing to grow

"As iron sharpens iron, so one man sharpens another."–Proverbs 27:17 (NIV)

7. Stay in the Fight and Keep Growing

You'll still face temptation, struggles, and spiritual warfare. But you don't face them alone. Stay grounded in Scripture, anchored in prayer, and connected to godly men.

3 Daily Habits to Build Now:

1. Spend time in the Word (even 10 minutes counts)
2. Pray (throughout your day, not just once)
3. Stay connected to other believers

Keep learning. Keep repenting. Keep following Jesus—one faithful step at a time.

8. Tell Someone

Share your decision with a friend, mentor, pastor, or family member. Don't keep it private. Telling someone strengthens your commitment and opens the door for support and encouragement.

"If you declare with your mouth, 'Jesus is Lord,' and believe in your heart… you will be saved." –Romans 10:9 (NIV)

You Are Not Who You Were

By accepting Jesus Christ as your Lord and Savior, you've embarked on a transformative journey. You are now forgiven, redeemed, and chosen. The Holy Spirit has sealed you, marking the beginning of a new life in Christ. Although this is the end of the book, it is not the end for you but the commencement of a lifelong adventure of faith and growth.

As Philippians 1:6 assures us, *"Being confident of this, that He who began a good work in you will carry it on to completion until the day of Christ Jesus."*

This verse reminds us that the work God has started in you is ongoing. He is committed to molding you into the image of His Son, guiding you through every challenge and triumph.

Embrace this new identity with confidence. You are a warrior in God's kingdom, equipped with His Word, empowered by His Spirit, and supported by a community of believers. Stay rooted in Scripture, remain steadfast in prayer, and seek fellowship with other Christians. These practices will fortify your faith and prepare you for the battles ahead.

Remember, transformation is a process. There will be moments of doubt and struggle, but take heart in knowing that God is with you every step of the way. He is faithful, and His promises are true. Lean on Him, and He will continue to work in you, shaping you into the man He has called you to be.

Welcome to the journey. Welcome to the brotherhood. Welcome to a new life in Christ.

APPENDIX: Prayers

Introduction to the Prayers

Prayer is the lifeblood of a man's spiritual journey and is a direct line to the heart of God. It's where battles are fought, victories are claimed, and transformation begins.

In the quiet moments of communion with our Creator, we find the strength to face trials, the wisdom to lead, and the courage to pursue our divine purpose.

This collection of prayers is crafted to accompany you through various facets of your walk with God. Whether you're seeking renewal, strength, clarity, brotherhood, or endurance, these prayers are designed to align your heart with God's will and empower you to live as the warrior He has called you to be.

Use these prayers as daily affirmations, battle cries in times of struggle, or meditations to deepen your relationship with the Lord. Let them serve as a foundation upon which you build a life of spiritual power and purpose.

Remember, a warrior is not defined by the battles he avoids but by the ones he engages with faith and perseverance. May these prayers equip you to stand firm, fight valiantly, and finish your race well.

Prayer Before Reading the Bible

Heavenly Father, Thank You for the gift of Your Word.
I come before You today with a heart that is open, ready, and eager to hear from You. I know that Your Word is alive, powerful, and able to transform my life. Please speak to me through Your Scriptures today.

Help me to understand Your truths, to apply them to my life, and to grow closer to You through every verse I read.
I pray that Your Holy Spirit would guide me, illuminate my heart, and give me wisdom as I read Your Word.

I ask for clarity to understand, strength to obey, and a deeper desire to live out what I learn.
Let Your Word convict me, encourage me, and mold me into the man You've called me to be.

Thank You for the opportunity to spend this time with You.
I trust that You will speak to me, and I am ready to receive all that You have for me today.

In Jesus' name,
Amen.

Morning Prayer

Father God, Thank You for waking me up today and giving me the gift of a new morning.
Your mercies are new, and Your grace is more than enough for whatever this day brings.

Before anything else, I surrender this day to You.
Lead me. Guide me. Strengthen me. Help me walk in step with Your Spirit, not my own strength.

Guard my thoughts, my words, and my actions. Help me honor You in every conversation, decision, and opportunity. Give me wisdom when I'm uncertain, patience when I'm tested, and boldness when I need to stand firm.

Help me see others the way You see them.
Help me serve with humility, love with sincerity, and lead with integrity.

Whatever comes today—success, pressure, opportunity, or trial—remind me that I'm not alone.
You are with me. You are for me. And You are working through me.

Thank You for being my strength, my peace, and my Provider.
Let today be a day that brings glory to Your name.

In Jesus' name,
Amen.

Evening Prayer

Heavenly Father, Thank You for walking with me through this day. Whether it was easy or hard, victorious or heavy, I know You were present in it all.

I pause now to breathe, to reflect, and to give this day back to You.

If I fell short today, I confess it and receive Your forgiveness.
If I carried stress, fear, or frustration, I release it into Your hands.
Wash my mind with Your peace and calm my heart with Your presence.

Thank You for the blessings I noticed and the ones I missed.

Thank You for protecting me, guiding me, and providing for me again.

Thank You for Your grace that carried me from morning to night.

As I rest tonight, guard my heart and my thoughts.
Speak to me in the quiet. Restore my strength.
Prepare me for tomorrow, and help me wake with a heart that's ready to follow You again.

You are my refuge. You are my Shepherd. You are always good.

In Jesus' name,
Amen.

Prayer for a Renewed Heart

Heavenly Father, I come before You with a heart that longs for transformation. I acknowledge my shortcomings and the ways I've strayed from Your path. Your Word says in Psalm 51:10, "Create in me a clean heart, O God, and renew a steadfast spirit within me." Lord, I echo this plea.

Cleanse me from all unrighteousness. Wash away the guilt, shame, and burdens that weigh me down. Replace my hardened heart with one that is tender and responsive to Your guidance.

Renew my mind, that I may think thoughts that are pure, noble, and aligned with Your truth. Strengthen my spirit, so I can stand firm against temptation and walk in obedience to Your commands.

Lord, I desire to be a vessel for Your purposes. Mold me, shape me, and use me to reflect Your love and grace to those around me. Let my life be a testament to Your redeeming power.

Thank You for Your mercy and for the promise that if we confess our sins, You are faithful and just to forgive us and purify us from all unrighteousness (1 John 1:9). I receive Your forgiveness and commit to walking in the newness of life that You offer.

In Jesus' name, Amen.

Prayer for Spiritual Strength

Heavenly Father, I bow before You, acknowledging that every family in heaven and on earth derives its name from You. I pray that, according to the riches of Your glory, You may strengthen me with power through Your Spirit in my inner being.

May Christ dwell in my heart through faith, that I, being rooted and grounded in love, may have the strength to comprehend with all the saints what is the breadth and length and height and depth of Your love.

Help me to know the love of Christ that surpasses knowledge, that I may be filled with all the fullness of God.

Lord, in moments of weakness, grant me Your strength. When I face trials and challenges, remind me that Your power is made perfect in my weakness. Empower me to stand firm in faith, to resist temptation, and to live a life that honors You.

Thank You for Your unfailing love and for the promise that You are able to do immeasurably more than all I can ask or imagine, according to Your power that is at work within me.

To You be glory in the church and in Christ Jesus throughout all generations, forever and ever.

In Jesus' name, Amen.

Prayer for Purpose and Direction

Heavenly Father, I come before You with a heart open to Your guidance. In the midst of life's uncertainties, I seek the clarity that only You can provide. Illuminate the path You have set for me, and grant me the wisdom to discern Your will in every decision I face.

Lord, I acknowledge that my understanding is limited, but Your knowledge is infinite. Help me to trust in Your timing and to remain patient as You unfold Your plan for my life. When doubts arise, strengthen my faith; when fear threatens to paralyze me, fill me with courage.

Reveal to me the unique purpose You have designed for me. Show me how to use the gifts and talents You've bestowed upon me to serve others and to glorify Your name. May my actions and behavior reflect Your love, and may my life be a demonstration of Your grace.

In moments of confusion and frustration, remind me of Your promises. When the road ahead seems unclear, be the lamp unto my feet and the light unto my path. Guide me through the valleys and over the mountains, knowing that with You, I am never alone.

Thank You, Lord, for Your unwavering love. I surrender my plans to You, trusting that Your purpose for me is greater than anything I could envision. Lead me, Father, into the destiny You have prepared, and may I walk in obedience and faith all the days of my life.

In Jesus' name, Amen.

Prayer for Brotherhood and Accountability

Heavenly Father, I come before You with a heart yearning for authentic brotherhood and the strength that comes from walking alongside fellow believers. You have created us not to journey alone but to thrive in community, sharpening one another as iron sharpens iron.

Lord, I confess that pride and fear have often kept me isolated. I have hesitated to share my struggles, fearing judgment or rejection. But I know that true freedom is found in vulnerability and that healing comes when we walk in the light together.

I ask You to bring into my life godly men who will stand with me in truth and love. Men who will hold me accountable, encourage me in my faith, and challenge me to grow. Help me to be that brother for others, offering grace and truth as we pursue You together.

Teach us to build relationships rooted in Your Word, where we can confess our sins, pray for one another, and spur each other on toward love and good deeds. May our fellowship be a reflection of Your love, drawing others to the hope we have in Christ.

Strengthen our bonds, Lord, so that we may stand firm against the schemes of the enemy. Let our unity be a testimony to the world of Your transforming power.

In Jesus' name, Amen.

Prayer for Endurance in Trials

Heavenly Father, I come before You acknowledging the weight of the trials I face. Life's challenges press heavily upon me, and at times, I feel overwhelmed. Yet, I know that You are my refuge and strength, an ever-present help in trouble. Therefore, I will not fear, even when the earth gives way and the mountains fall into the heart of the sea.

Lord, I ask for the endurance to persevere through these hardships. Strengthen my spirit when I am weary, and renew my hope when I feel discouraged. Help me to trust in Your unfailing love and to remember that these trials are shaping me, refining my character, and drawing me closer to You.

Teach me to rejoice in suffering, knowing that suffering produces perseverance; perseverance, character; and character, hope. Let this hope anchor my soul, firm and secure, as I navigate the storms of life.

Father, grant me the wisdom to see each challenge as an opportunity to grow in faith. Surround me with a community of believers who can support and encourage me, and help me to be a source of strength for others in their times of need.

I surrender my burdens to You, Lord, casting all my anxieties on You, because You care for me. Fill me with Your peace that surpasses all understanding, guarding my heart and mind in Christ Jesus.

In every trial, may I fix my eyes on Jesus, the author and perfecter of my faith, who endured the cross for the joy set before Him. Let His example inspire me to run with perseverance the race marked out for me.

Thank You, Lord, for Your constant presence and for the promise that You will never leave me nor forsake me. I place my trust in You, confident that You will carry me through every hardship. In Jesus' name, Amen.

Prayer for Spiritual Warfare

Heavenly Father,

Thank You that in Christ, I am not fighting for victory. I am fighting from it.

You have already defeated the enemy through the cross and the empty tomb, and You have given me everything I need to stand strong today.

Right now, I put on the full armor of God:

- The **belt of truth** to stand against lies and deception
- The **breastplate of righteousness** to guard my heart from compromise
- The **shoes of the gospel of peace** to stay grounded in Your mission
- The **shield of faith** to extinguish every flaming arrow of doubt, fear, or temptation
- The **helmet of salvation** to protect my mind and remind me who I am in Christ
- The **sword of the Spirit** which is Your Word, alive and powerful in my hands

Lord, make me alert today. Help me recognize the enemy's tactics.

Where he whispers shame, remind me of Your grace.

Where he tempts me to fear, strengthen my faith.

Where he tries to divide, give me a spirit of unity and love.

Where he accuses, remind me that I am forgiven, redeemed, and sealed by Your Spirit.

I resist the devil in Jesus' name, and I declare that no weapon formed against me will prosper.

I plead the blood of Jesus over my mind, my home, my family, my relationships, and my future.

Fill me with boldness. Fill me with discernment. Fill me with the power of Your Holy Spirit. I do not stand in my strength. I stand in Yours, and I will not retreat. I will not compromise. I will not give the enemy ground.

Today, I fight as a son of the King.
Today, I walk in freedom, with authority and confidence.
Today, I stand.

In the mighty name of Jesus, Amen.

www.ingramcontent.com/pod-product-compliance
Lightning Source LLC
Chambersburg PA
CBHW050634160426
43194CB00010B/1671